W9-CDH-117

The Shotgun Handbook

Mike George

The Crowood Press

First published in 1998 by
The Crowood Press Ltd
Ramsbury, Marlborough
Wiltshire SN8 2HR

© Mike George 1998

All rights reserved. No part of this publication may be reproduced or transmitted
in any form or by any means, electronic or mechanical, including photocopy,
recording, or any information storage and retrieval system, without permission in
writing from the publishers.

British Library Cataloguing-in-Publication Data

A catalogue record for this book is available from the British Library.

ISBN 1 86126 157 8

Dedication
To the four ladies in my life. My late mother Sylvia, who encouraged me to
study engineering despite my decision to become a journalist; to my sister Mary,
who taught me about computer-controlled machine tools; and to my step-daughter Shona,
whose youthful zest for life always inspires; and, of course, to my wife Pringle, the
Scottish lassie who was brave enough to marry me when we were both old enough to
know better, who couldn't hit a barn door at ten paces with a skeet gun, who cooks game
like a Cordon Bleu chef, who understands what I call 'creative moods' and she calls bad
temper, and who constantly defends our rights to shoot and fish although she does neither.
God bless 'em all!

Note
Safety is of the utmost importance in every aspect of shotgun work and gun handling.
Throughout this book I have tried very hard and constantly to recommend safe procedures.
However, neither I nor the publisher can accept any responsibility for any accident or injury
caused by following the advice given.

Printed and bound in Great Britain by The Bath Press, Bath

CONTENTS

INTRODUCTION

Whether you think of the modern shotgun as a working tool or a work of art, how it works – or at least how it ought to work – is a source of constant fascination to all who shoot. Like all sportsmen, shotgun shooters seek constantly to improve their performance, and choosing the right gun, then further improving it to suit individual needs, is an important part of the process.

Choosing a gun, new or second-hand, is an exciting but sometimes confusing experience made no easier, as in other aspects of life, by advertising claims, rumour and the often endless advice of well-meaning friends. Sorting out problems with guns can be another source of great confusion and I have often been asked whether I can recommend a book on the subject. In truth, I have never been able to do so. The only answer was to write one, and in it I have tried to put down, in a reasonably logical order, exactly what I have learned about the subject over many years.

In the book I have tried to throw out a lot of old ideas and to start afresh with an in-depth look at the type of gun most of us shoot – the modern over-and-under, with a little about the semi-auto. Too many books, I feel, are hidebound by the lore and legend of the traditional, British side-by-side, which has become rarer as the years have gone by. I have also tried to get rid of the idea that 'hand-made is best', because in our terms it isn't – we need well-made guns at prices we can afford. Our guns, like the cars we drive, are made by machine tools in modern factories.

I have also had a look at how modern ammunition is made and at the ever-important question of recoil and how we can reduce it to manageable proportions, on the grounds that shooting is supposed to be a pleasure rather than a pain in the shoulder.

In fact, pleasure is what shooting is all about, and my greatest wish is that this book should help you to enjoy your shooting sport all the more.

My thanks go to all those unsung heroes in the gun trade: to Robin Scott and Rob Hardy of Sporting Gun, to Vere and Leon Richardson at Richardsons' Gun Shop in Halesworth, to Jason Harris, to Roger Hancox and his expert crew at the Birmingham Proof House, to Dave Allen at the Hull Cartridge Co., to Jim Silvestri at Trap and Field Supplies in Morayshire, to David Baker, Sporting Gun's gun historian, to my engineering instructor Ron Holloway, to Malcolm Cooper of Accuracy International, and to the late Frank Marriott who supervised my first-ever shot when I was 14 years old. Down the years all these people and many more have given me much help and encouragement.

Mike George
Portgordon
Scotland
December 1997

1 A CHANGING PATTERN

Over the last twenty years the British shotgun shooter has experienced a dramatic rethinking of the design and style of his gun. That is surprising when you consider that nothing to enhance significantly the performance of the shotgun has appeared for around a hundred years, yet preferences have changed in just one generation.

SIDE-BY-SIDE TO OVER-AND-UNDER

No longer does the British shooter always carry the traditional side-by-side. It has been generally forsaken for the over-and-under, and all but a few hand-built exotics, costing at least as much as the average man earns in a year, are built not in Britain but overseas. The reasons form a fascinating tale, as much to do with the changing patterns of British manufacturing and trade as they are with the elements of good design; yet the fact remains that there has been a revolution in thinking.

When I edited the very first issue of *Sporting Gun* back in the mid-1970s it was at the end of the 'traditional' era, and the most common shotgun in Britain was still the side-by-side. Its basic design was unchanged from the end of the last century, and only its country of origin was different. The British gun trade – or at least the popular, affordable end of it – had died because it had failed to live with the changing times. It is easy to criticize with hindsight, but it was a self-inflicted wound brought about by under-financing, ultra-conservative thinking and a failure to invest in the machine tools and working practices which were the keys to future prosperity in all engineering disciplines.

The problem was that shotgun-making was still thought of as a hand craft rather than as mass-production engineering. The gun trade was, and still is, keen to promote the idea that guns are made or at least finished by hand, a time-consuming, labour-intensive practice which had no part in modern engineering. 'Machine-made' was promoted as 'inferior', in a period when machines were beating traditional craft practices for precision hands-down. What is more, the more you use machines for every aspect of gun manufacture, the greater the interchangeability of parts you get – guns can be repaired with parts off the shelf, with no hand-fettling to make them fit. The British gun trade was to pay dearly for this old-fashioned thinking.

THE GROWTH IN IMPORTED GUNS

Famous names in the Birmingham gun trade – Britain's traditional source of cheap and medium-priced guns – had been through a period of dramatic decline from which they would never recover, and gun dealers were looking to Europe and elsewhere for guns that the average enthusiast could afford. At first British gun traders looked abroad for English side-by-side look-alikes, and a far-seeing importer took advantage of Spain's traditional craftsmanship and undeveloped economy to bring in affordable guns that handled and balanced like the English favourites. They were well built and available at the right price, and thus the great landslide of importing began.

In the early days of mass importing foreign guns were so cheap because craftsmen in

European countries such as Spain and Italy demanded lower wages than their British counterparts, were prepared to work longer hours, and the pound was strong. At that time you could stay in a good hotel in an Italian city for little more than £1 a night, and holidays in Spain were phenomenally cheap. Guns from the old Communist bloc states were cheaper still than those from western Europe because their governments paid their workers even less, and were desperate for hard currency at almost any price to bolster their flagging economies.

That economic pattern gradually faded as the European Community got into gear and Communist bloc started to crumble. But, unlike the British gun trade, European manufacturers invested in modern tooling which brought its own economies. They were not hidebound by the labour-intensive practices which were the curse of the British gun trade.

A present-day, affordable gun from an overseas manufacturer is not the carefully handcrafted item some people in the trade would still like you to think it is, but the result of developments in precise, computer-controlled machine tools and the employment of a minimum number of highly trained engineers. This is not unique to the gun trade – the same pattern is evident in all other forms of production engineering. Cars are built by robots and advertised as being better for it. Successful gun companies keep hand-fitting and finishing to an absolute minimum.

Nowadays, if you seek hand-built perfection, the quality of top-grade English shotguns such as those from Purdey, Boss, Holland & Holland and a number of smaller firms, is finer than ever – with prices to match. Gunmaking as an art rather than a strict science still flourishes, and long may it do so for those who can afford it. But the average shooter with between £500 and £5,000 to spend shoots an import because, if he wants a new gun, he has no other choice. There is just no British-made alternative and neither is there likely to be while the manufacturing arm of our gun trade chooses to live in the past.

ENTER THE OVER-AND-UNDER

Despite popular belief, the over-and-under (O/U) was not invented by John Moses Browning. His famous B25 design of 1925 – still an international yardstick for O/U design and quality – represented not so much original thought as a fastidious engineer's wish to create the ultimate of its type. English makers had been building fine O/U shotguns and double rifles since the late 1800s. Woodward's design of 1913 – later taken on by Purdey – was particularly elegant in both its aesthetics and engineering, but the design never really caught the trade's enthusiasm. Edwardian Britain was, in general, far too conservative. The great game shots of the era – mainly the titled and the wealthy – preferred their traditional handmade side-by-sides and their preferences were copied by those further down the then-strict social scale. Keepers and ordinary, working-class shooters followed the example of their masters and bought the 'best' side-by-side look-alikes or the nearest to them that they could afford.

It was Browning who popularized the type in both Europe and America with his B25, and it finally began to sell in Britain on the back of its international clay-shooting successes. It was a trend which was to become hugely significant in the late 1970s and the early 1980s. Most 'new' shooters in the last twenty years and more have come into the sport through clay shooting which was developing from a minority interest – often just off-season practice for 'the real thing' – into a sport of the people in its own right, and, when the participants progressed to field shooting, they took their gun design preferences, and often the same gun, with them.

The O/U, although it parted with tradition, was, with its single sighting plane and uncluttered sight picture, a much more 'pointable' gun and its virtues were soon realized in all branches of the shotgun shooting sports. It was altogether a handier tool and the new breed of shooters – many from urban rather than country backgrounds – had no preconceived notions as to what a shotgun should be. Like their clay-shooting heroes, they wanted to shoot an O/U and, in the early days, an O/U that looked like a Browning.

This is not to say the O/U was not without its critics, and for many years there was something not quite 'gentlemanly' about bringing an O/U to a smart game shoot. Even in the 1980s more than one guest was sent home and told to come back with 'a gun on which the barrels had been assembled the right way round' if he wanted to take part in the day's sport. However, in a changing society such conservatism was on the way out for good.

Overseas gunmakers found themselves with a growing market – and a dilemma. The O/U was no cheaper to produce than the side-by-side and manufacturing costs through most of Europe were beginning to spiral. The whole problem is typified by the Browning B25, which was and still is built in Belgium. Put bluntly, it had become an engineer's worst nightmare. In its heyday John Moses claimed that it was made of twenty-two different types of steel and the eighty-four parts were subjected to 794 precision operations, while sixty-seven parts had different heat treatments. The parts were checked by 1,490 instruments and gauges, which performed 2,310 different checks and measurements. Craftsmen performed 155 different hand operations. It was a Rolls-Royce of a gun trying to compete in a growing Ford market. The statistics had made convincing advertising in the era when 'hand' work was thought of as vastly superior to even the most accurate machining; but the B25 was over-engineered, labour-intensive in production, and had to sell at an ever-increasing price.

AUTOMATE FOR SUCCESS

Browning needed cheaper guns in order to remain a world player, so they turned to Miroku of Japan for their mainstream manufacture. The American giant Winchester had also been involved with Japan since the 1960s for the production of their world-market O/U, and thus the Far East joined mainland Europe as the replacement for the all-but-dead British gun-manufacturing trade. The Italian giant Beretta – the other major player in the world – had managed to keep its production in the home country through wise investments in economic tooling and carefully researched market slots for its products.

It must be said that there lies the key to the matter. Successful gun mass-manufacturers – sadly none of them British – are those who have automated their processes to produce guns which handle well, point nicely, shoot straight, look elegant and sell at competitive prices. The term 'factory-made gun' was once almost an insult, implying a lack of craftsmanship and even crudeness. Now all affordable guns are 'factory-made', and – like those cars assembled by robots – many of them are all the better for it. In fact, the modern, factory-made O/U has developed into two distinctly different subdesigns, one owing its basic layout to the Browning and the other to the Beretta or, if you prefer, to the Purdey/Woodward.

The Browning Version

Put simply, the Browning style, typified by modern, Japanese-built Brownings, Mirokus and the late, much-lamented Winchester 101, employs a full-width hinge pin which runs immediately beneath the front of the chamber of the lower barrel. This leads to a relatively deep action, so that there is plenty of space for the designer to stack all of the gun's mechanical features neatly and logically one on top of another. The locking bolt runs along the bottom of the action, where its forward end can locate with a relatively deep slot or bite on a generous lump built on to the bottom of the lower barrel. The firing mechanism is on top of that, with the tumblers or hammers hinged on the trigger plate and the sears hinged from the top strap. From the point of view of depth there is still plenty of space inside this action.

Its critics say that this style of action is not as mechanically efficient as it should be. The locking bolt, being rather a long way from the top

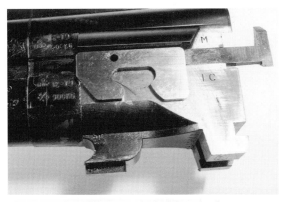

Ejectors such as this are typical of those used on Brownings, Mirokus and the now-discontinued Winchesters. The mechanism is actuated by kickers built into the fore-end iron.

Most guns are locked closed by the bolt getting a firm hold on this bite, cut into the barrel lumps.

On a gun with a full-width hinge pin this is what is known as the hook – the part of the barrel lump which fits around the pin.

barrel, allows unnecessary mechanical stresses to build up in the gun, and the recoil is not transmitted as straight back along the line of the stock as it might be. In pure engineering terms this may be true, but the design is still strong enough to be entirely safe and to have a long life, and there are other factors of equal importance, the handling characteristics, for instance. We look at those in a later chapter.

The Italian Job

I tend to refer to the alternative design as the 'Italian school' because, although it was not invented by them, it typifies the modern Italian shotgun. Beretta and Perazzi guns, and a host of generally cheaper alternatives, are built on these principles. The idea of these Italian design principles is to make the action more shallow and therefore to redistribute firing stresses more favourably and to transmit recoil back down the stock in a straighter line. The first design principle involves getting rid of the full-width hinge pin under the lower barrel and hinging the barrels on short stub pins let into the action walls. These stub pins, like steel buttons, engage with semi-circular cut-outs in the walls of the lower barrel and thus form the hinge. This arrangement moves the hinge axis upwards by around $1/2$in (12mm) and therefore gives the potential to make the action that much shallower – provided that the manufacturer can think of something imaginative to do with the locking bolt.

Beretta have an elegant answer to this problem. Instead of making a full-width bolt, they employ a component of two-pronged fork shape and mount it high in the action, just below the centre point of the upper barrel. The cone-shaped ends of the fork 'prongs' pass through holes in the face of the standing breech and, when the gun is closed, engage with a pair of cone-shaped holes machined into the barrel shoulders. This allows for a very shallow action and results in a neat, rounded shape to the inside of the action floor. The action is mechanically very strong, as well as being elegant in appearance and easy to clean. It is probably easier and cheaper to machine too.

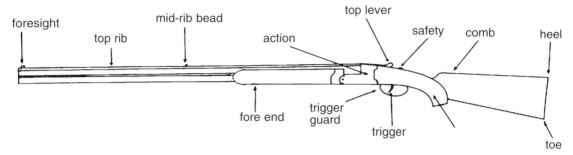

The general arrangement of a typical over-and-under shotgun. This particular gun has a low-profile action hinged to the barrels by stub pins.

The Beretta bolting system consists of two stout pins which are part of a fork-shaped bolt. They project through the breech face and locate with holes in the barrel shoulder. Also visible is the top firing pin and the button which releases the top lever when the gun is closed.

These two holes, in the barrel shoulders of a Beretta, receive the tips of the fork-shaped bolt which secures the gun closed.

Internal stub pins such as this form the hinge in a gun with a low-level action.

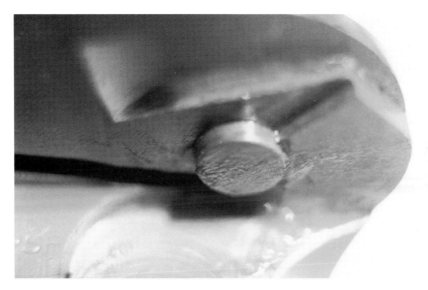

Stub pins locate with semi-circular cut-outs on the forward part of the barrel lump.

Other manufacturers do things differently and leave the bolt in its traditional position, running along the action floor. Economies of depth are achieved by making the barrel lump very shallow indeed and cutting the location slot, or 'bite', for the bolt tip as close as possible to the lower edge of the bottom chamber. This variation is generally not quite as shallow as in the Beretta style but has similar advantages in stress distribution.

Shallow actions often have both tumblers and sears mounted on the trigger plate, and Perazzi take this design feature to its ultimate by building the trigger and the tumbler mechanism as a separate, drop-out unit, a feature which is also available on some Beretta, Krieghoff and Franchi models, the Spanish-built Kemen, and the hand-built British Holland & Holland, if you have that kind of money. As a general rule, but not always, shallow-action guns have spring-loaded ejectors in which the bulk of the mechanism is contained within the action and the

Most shotguns with low-level actions have spring-loaded ejectors, as typified by the mechanisms on this Italian-built Fabarm.

Stub pins often have decorated heads. Nevertheless, they can usually be removed and replaced.

chamber walls. Deep-action, Browning-style guns usually have two-piece ejectors, with separate kickers and springs attached to the fore-end iron and enclosed by the wood. There is no difference in efficiency between these two mechanisms, although the spring-loaded design has fewer parts and so offers engineering economies and there is therefore less to go wrong.

Both of these styles of O/U can – at the expense of quite a lot of hand fitting – be built to a sidelock design in which the lock mecha-nisms are built on to separate, removable lock plates. Browning have never built a B25 side-lock, but the sidelock Beretta SO series is high-ly successful. AYA of Spain have built a sidelock version of their Coral O/U design, and a similar gun from Germany – the Merkel – is also avail-able with the detachable lock plates. However, the advantages of this style are negligible in mechanical terms – in fact, it may be argued that sidelocks will not generally stand up to many years of repeated firing in the same way as boxlocks. Added to which sidelock prices are high, generally twice as much or more than those of the equivalent gun in boxlock format. In everyday shooting terms, the sidelock remains a rich man's plaything – certainly elegant, but arguably poor value in strictly practical, value-for-money terms.

ROLL OUT THE BARREL

One mechanical feature most O/U shotguns now share is the method of barrel construction. There was a time when quality shotgun barrels were manufactured as two separate tubes with – on a side-by-side – the lumps forged in at the breech end. Each tube, and its half of the lump, was thus made of one single piece of steel, a feature which imparted great strength. This was known as building on the 'chopper lump' principle because each tube, in profile, looked rather like an axe, and it was applied to the O/U design by forging the complete lump as part of the lower barrel. In both designs the two tubes were then soldered together to form one unit; traditionally with soft, lead-based solder and more recently with mechanically stronger brazing alloys and silver solders.

In engineering terms this was irksome, in that the barrels had to be forged as solid bars which then had to be bored out, and once bored they became difficult to handle on machine tools. Again, much undesirable hand work was involved and there had to be a way which would impart just as much strength as the traditional design and be more economical to produce. The answer was found in what is called the 'monobloc' system. With this method the chamber ends of both barrels, and the lump, are machined from a single forging which is strong and easily gripped through successive machining processes. Later the tubes are sleeved in and locked permanently in position with modern brazing alloys. The principle can be used on side-by-sides as well as O/Us and is now used in most gun factories throughout the world. Miroku, who stayed with chopper-lump construction longer than most, abandoned it when they invested in a new barrel plant. They claimed that, with a coming world-wide requirement for steel shot, the new barrels were stronger. Be that as it may, the new barrel sets must also have been cheaper to produce.

On other gun parts manufacturers now use high-precision die castings, laser and spark-erosion cutting, CNC (computer numerical control) machining centres: the full range of modern machining techniques. They bring ease of manufacture and a further bonus for the gun owner – the previously-mentioned interchangeability of parts.

The precision manufacturing of actions has allowed far more automation in the production of gun woodwork. Stocks and fore-ends are now made on high-speed profile cutters and they tend to fit with little or no hand work, another bonus for the shooter. In fact, only tradition demands that we continue to use wood at all and modern engineering plastics are waiting in the wings. They may not look as elegant as fine walnut but they are far stronger, easier to keep clean and are totally unaffected by changes in temperature and humidity.

Does all this mean that the gun has become a mere shooting machine rather than a thing of beauty? To my mind it does not: elegance is a matter of appearance rather than the method of manufacture. A car does not have to be hand-made in order to look elegant and neither does a gun. And, although hand-built excellence and individuality will continue to rise in price as the years go by, there will always be customers for them. The fine traditions of custom gun-smithing – beautifying the ordinary and improving its mechanical parts and method of operation to individual requirements – are on safe ground too.

2 CHOOSING THE GUN FOR THE JOB

Shotguns are rather like golf clubs: what's right for one kind of shot is not necessarily right for another. You would not expect a golfer to play every shot in eighteen holes with the same club, and neither would you enter a Grand Prix with a family saloon. By the same token you cannot shoot every discipline with the same shotgun – a point our legislators should remember when framing future laws.

You can buy an all-purpose gun which is 'nearly right' for everything, but if you are to pursue the shooting sports seriously, then each group of disciplines requires its own, specialized gun. Each type has evolved over the years to become what it is today, and it is a process of constant evolution. Guns change with the times, sometimes because of fashion and sometimes because of genuine improvement. These changes will continue, as we shall see.

The main differences between guns for the different disciplines are in barrel length, weight, stock design and where the shot pattern strikes in relation to the aiming point. There are other, minor differences and many of the designs are compromises built around the rules or practicalities of the particular shooting sport for which the different guns are designed. Let us have a detailed look at these types.

THE SPORTER

The Sporter began its life as a particularly British creation, despite the fact that most were and are still manufactured abroad. The reason is simple: throughout the rest of the world the most popular competition disciplines are trap and skeet, while Sporting, a simulation of the

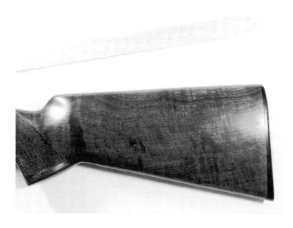

This Sporter stock has typical drops at comb and heel. The ruler is in line with the sight plane.

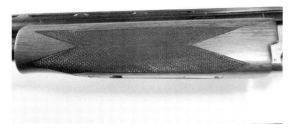

This fore-end is a popular design of a Sporter: slim and nicely curved.

types of shot encountered in field shooting, is Britain's most popular shooting game. We invented it, or at least developed it as a serious discipline, and we also soon discovered the right specifications for the gun to shoot it. Only in recent years has the discipline spread to the world's biggest gun market – the USA – and there is still only a minority following in continental Europe. Drive through rural France and you will see plenty of signs to 'Le Ball Trap', and the multiplicity of trap layouts in Italy are among the best in the world, but Sporting is still only shot by the few outside the United Kingdom.

It took some time for British importers to knock this fact into the heads of European gun manufacturers and, as a result, many of the earlier Sporters were trap guns in disguise; they tended to be over-heavy, with stocks which were far too high for the demands of the discipline. Only the barrels were different, with chokes bored out to shoot slightly wider patterns. Many of today's successful Sporters are a direct result of pressure put on manufacturers by British importers to produce guns which are right for the game, instead of a 'nearly right' compromise.

The ideal Sporter still has to be a gun of compromises in some respects: heavy and steady enough to soak up the recoil of repeated firing and for considered shots against distant targets, yet fast and lively enough for quicker, closer clays presented at cunning angles. It must tackle outgoing, incoming, crossing and quartering targets with equal facility and be capable of being mounted to the shoulder in a very slick fashion.

These requirements are usually translated into a gun with 30in barrels and an all-up weight of around $7^3/_4$lb, although the choice of any barrel length between 28 and 32in is totally acceptable if it suits the shooter's individual preference or style. Most guns are multichokes, but if it is a fixed-choke it will be choked $^1/_4$ and $^1/_2$, or thereabouts. It must have a barrel selector so that the shooter can choose which barrel to fire first, because pairs of targets often consist of a distant clay followed by a close one, and you would not want to be shooting a distant target with a lightly choked barrel. It will balance either on the hinge pin or no more than about

$^3/_8$ in in front of it, and the main weight of the gun will be built into the area between the midpoint of the fore-end and the pistol grip: the area which falls between the hands. These are the features which give fast handling when it is required: make a gun with heavy muzzles and bring it back to balance by weighting the rear of the stock and the gun does not move and point as quickly.

The rib is usually no wider than $^3/_8$in (10mm) and may be either parallel to or slightly tapering towards the muzzle end. It will terminate in a small bead foresight, the colour of the shooter's choice, and there is no need for a mid-rib bead.

Woodwork styles and dimensions are important. The fore-end is usually slim and of schnabel shape, while the pistol grip has an easy curve and no palm swell. Drops at comb and heel of $1^1/_2$ and $2^1/_2$in or thereabouts suit most people of average build. The stock will be fitted with a buttplate of hard plastic, wood or relatively hard rubber with a shiny surface so that it does not snag on clothing when the gun is mounted. To further help in this regard many guns have the top of the heel angled off or rounded. This buttplate really is important: one that drags on clothing may cost you many targets in the course of a competition.

A combination of stock dimensions and rib

The Sporter Specification

Barrels: 30in (or to shooter's individual choice); multichoke or $^1/_4$ and $^1/_2$ fixed-choke; 10mm parallel or slightly tapering rib; small bead foresight; $2^3/_4$in (70mm) chambers.

Action: boxlock or sidelock; single selective trigger; non-automatic safety.

Stock: pistol grip; length $14^3/_8$in, $1^1/_2$in drop at comb, $2^1/_2$in drop at heel; cast and fine tuning of dimensions to suit the individual.

Fore-end: slim type, usually of schnabel form.

Weight: approximately $7^3/_4$lb.

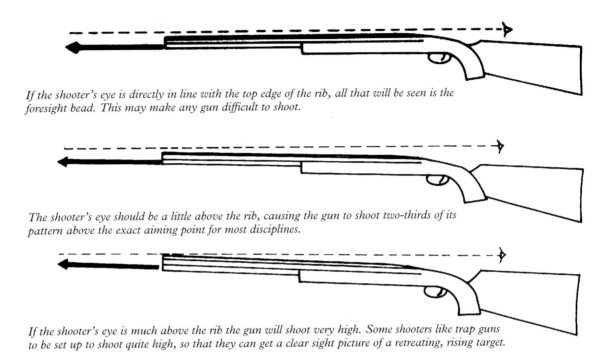

If the shooter's eye is directly in line with the top edge of the rib, all that will be seen is the foresight bead. This may make any gun difficult to shoot.

The shooter's eye should be a little above the rib, causing the gun to shoot two-thirds of its pattern above the exact aiming point for most disciplines.

If the shooter's eye is much above the rib the gun will shoot very high. Some shooters like trap guns to be set up to shoot quite high, so that they can get a clear sight picture of a retreating, rising target.

alignment should make the gun shoot two-thirds of its pattern above the aim point and one-third below. With most people this would allow a stationary target to be fired at and hit in the middle of the pattern with a sight picture showing about a $1/4$in of 'daylight' between the target and the sight bead.

THE SKEET GUN

Twenty years ago skeet was shot with a rather different gun to the one which is preferred now. Lightning-fast handling was thought to be absolutely essential for tackling the relatively close crossing targets and, to achieve this, weight was kept to a minimum and barrels were short. Typical of the breed was the skeet version of the Japanese-built Winchester 101. It had a $26^1/_2$in barrels and weighed $7^1/_4$lb. On the other side of the world Beretta and Franchi were building guns of similar weight and length and the configuration was thought to be ideal. Such guns were choked 'skeet and skeet', in other words with identical chokes in both barrels. Most manufacturers' designation of a skeet choke was anywhere between a true cylinder and an improved cylinder; in other words, from a completely parallel tube to a mere 0.005in of constriction. Another popular feature was the

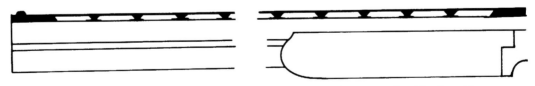

Ventilated ribs are usually fitted to Sporters and skeet guns. Widths vary, but are rarely wider than 13mm and may be parallel or tapering.

'retro-skeet' choke boring in which the shot passed through a vastly over-bored, short chamber before it entered the slight constriction of the choke itself. This was not to spread the pattern further, as was widely believed, but to elongate it in the air. With a long pattern, it was thought – quite rightly – that errors of lead were less important. If you shot far enough in front of the target the clay would run into the long shot string and be broken. With a long shot string, if you watch carefully, you can see a flying clay being 'nibbled away' from the front edge backwards, although it takes keen eyesight to do so because it all happens in a fraction of a second.

To understand how the skeet gun has evolved in Britain one first has to understand the differences in the discipline world-wide. Although few people do it, you may call for the target at English skeet with the gun ready mounted to the shoulder. Most people do not, preferring to wait with the gun just out of the shoulder. Olympic skeet is different. Not only are the targets faster, but the shooter has to call for the clay with the stock at waist level, and the gun may not be moved until the clay leaves the trap. American skeet targets are about as fast as the English and you may call for a target with the gun ready mounted; but the Americans shoot Station Eight, which is right in the middle of the range, between the two houses. From this peg targets are shot at very close range and very fast reactions are required.

From this brief description it may be seen that at English skeet the shooter can benefit from using a slightly slower gun, giving a steadier and more positive swing. The emphasis can be on precision rather than ultra-high speed, and the result is that the skeet gun generally preferred in the United Kingdom is now, except in choking, little different from the Sporter. A weight of $7^3/_4$lb or slightly less is about right, and barrel lengths have crept up to 28 or 30in. In fact, many of the top English skeet experts now shoot Sporters. Ribs are generally up to $^1/_2$in (13mm) wide and parallel, and mid-rib beads offer little or no advantage.

The Sporter's ideal stock dimensions also suit the skeet gun. The sight picture of a clay $^1/_2$in above the rib is comfortable, leaving the shooter to concentrate on the problems of lead. And, again like the sporting shooter, the skeet shooter can mount the gun at the requisite speed if it is fitted with a buttplate made of a hard material, with a slightly angled or rounded heel.

Most skeet shooters still prefer chokes of between true cylinder and 0.005in. of constriction, although some top-ranking competitors find that chokes as tight as $^1/_4$ (0.010 of constriction) give slightly more positive breaks and therefore boost confidence. A ball of dust in the air always looks better than a clay flying on with a big chip out of it, although twenty-five chips are always better than twenty-four balls of dust and a miss!

A foresight may be either a spherical bead of brass or nickel, or a cylinder of opaque or translucent material held in black metal, the latter type is usually found on competition guns.

The Skeet Gun Specification

Barrels: 28–30in fixed-choke, choked skeet and skeet; 10 to 13mm parallel rib, small bead foresight, $2^3/_4$in (70mm) chambers.

Action: Boxlock or sidelock; single non-selective trigger.

Stock: Pistol grip; length $14^3/_8$in, $1^1/_2$in drop at comb, $2^1/_2$in drop at heel; cast and fine tuning of dimensions to suit individual.

Fore-end: Generally a semi-beavertail is preferred.

Weight: $7^3/_4$lb.

There is no reason for a skeet gun to be a multichoke, although some skeet competitors now shoot multichokes because they allow the use of non-standard choke tubes which may print superior patterns and reduce the perceived recoil and muzzle flip. And neither is there any need for the trigger mechanism to be selective. Both barrels have the same chokes, and always firing the bottom barrel first leads to a slightly faster second-target acquisition in the doubles.

View along the rib of a gun fitted with a mid-rib bead. The beads should form a figure of eight, with about 3/8in (10mm) of rib showing.

THE TRAP GUN

Trap shooting in its many forms is a game of outgoing targets which emerge around 16yd in front of the shooter. When shot at they are going away from him at angles within a prescribed arc and for the first half of their flight they are rising as well.

The rules of all the trap disciplines also allow the shooter to call for the target with the gun ready mounted to the shoulder. The shooter still needs to be able to swing with the flight of the target, but to a lesser degree than in other disciplines. However, the swing has to be extremely smooth and precise. All this calls for a particular type of gun which is not really suited to any other discipline.

To look at the requirements one by one: first, there is no need for the gun to be capable of slick, on-the-move mounting. Before the target is called for the shooter can settle the gun comfortably in the shoulder and place his eye in exactly the right position behind the rib, and so this is one discipline in which a relatively thick, soft recoil pad does no harm. In mounting the gun there is no requirement for speed, and you may as well be as comfortable as possible.

To tackle a rising target with, say, a Sporter, it would be necessary to aim the shot well over the top of it. This would involve lifting the gun through its flight line until it had disappeared behind the muzzles, which is no great handicap for the occasional trap-type or rising target on a Sporting course, but it provides an unnecessary one when every target is of this type. The remedy with a trap gun is to make it shoot higher than its point of aim, so that the shooter is able to keep the target in view at all times, with the comfortable sight picture of the clay hovering about $1/4$in above the foresight bead.

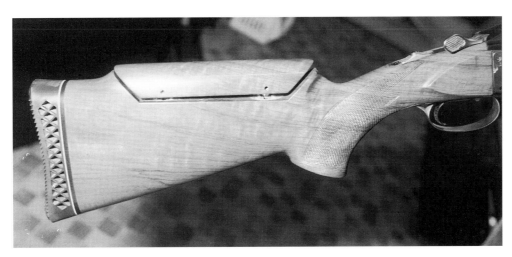

The stock of this trap gun – a top-quality Kreighoff – has an adjustable comb and a comfortable, ventilated recoil pad.

These targets are also more pleasant to shoot and are taken more accurately if the shooter can take the shot in a comfortable, relaxed, head-up position, without crouching his shoulders or bending his neck, yet still with the stock pressed comfortably into his cheek. For these reasons, the comb of the stock on trap guns is usually flatter and higher than on guns for other disciplines. The drop is usually about $3/16$in (4mm) higher at the comb and $3/8$in (10mm) higher at the heel. The rib/barrel alignment may differ slightly too, to make the shot go where the shooter desires.

In its general handling characteristics, the trap gun may also be somewhat steadier than other types. Rapid swings at crossing targets are not a requirement, while a little extra weight helps to soak up the recoil over the long strings of shots which are common in the discipline, as long as the gun is in balance. A good trap gun may be relatively heavy, but it should not feel so when it is held in the shooting position at the shoulder. A typical trap gun therefore weighs 8lb or more, and some of the best weigh $8 1/2$lb.

The kind of positive, steady swing which is desirable for trap also allows the use of long barrels, which are usually between 30 and 32in. Such barrels also give a desirable, longer sight base. Many shooters also find that a wide rib is helpful, and ribs of up to 16mm are common. High-raised ribs, with steep ramps at the back, are preferred by some shooters in order to achieve the desired head position.

In addition to a foresight, a small mid-rib bead is often fitted. If, on mounting a gun so fitted, the shooter observes the two beads in a perfect figure-of-eight formation, then the rib and the eye are perfectly aligned and the target may be called for.

When it is considered that the nearest shot at a trap target is going to be taken at around 30yd and a second shot at more than 40, chokes in a trap gun need to be tight. The normal layout is to have $3/4$ in the bottom barrel and full in the top, although for the tightly-patterning 24g ammunition used in the international disciplines some shooters prefer standard chokes to be eased out by about 0.005in. There is no need for a trap gun to have a barrel selector, as second shots always require a tighter choke because

The high ventilated rib, ramped at its rear end, is usually fitted only to trap guns and does not seem to be much in favour at present.

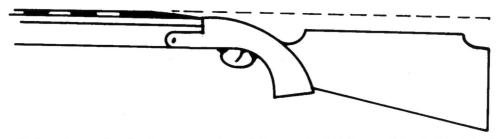

A Monte Carlo stock, sometimes fitted to trap guns, has a built-up comb which lies parallel to the line of the rib.

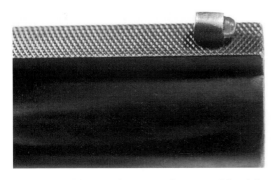

This competition gun has a translucent, red foresight bead, encased in a ring of metal.

This simple rib has been milled with a cross-hatched pattern to prevent glare when shooting on bright days.

This is another foresight alternative: a white bead encased in a metal ring.

This mid-rib bead is on a rib type which is quite common on competition guns; it has a central sight channel.

they are bound to be further away. Neither is there any requirement for a trap gun to be a

---

The Trap Gun Specification

Barrels: 30 to 32in, choked $^3/_4$ and full.

Rib: up to 16mm wide.

Small mid-rib bead: optional; $2^3/_4$in (70mm) chambers.

Action: boxlock or sidelock; single non-selective trigger.

Stock: length $14^3/_8$in; drop at comb $1^1/_8$in; drop at heel $2^1/_8$in or less; cast to suit shooter. Fore-end: beavertail or semi-beavertail.

Weight: 8lb or more.

---

multichoke, although in the past some have been produced with a multichoke tube in the bottom barrel.

THE GAME GUN

A game gun may be used for driven birds one day, walked-up game the next, then in a pigeon or duck hide, then for gamekeeping duties. In other words, it needs to have all the adaptability of the Sporter yet be light enough to be carried in the field all day without causing undue fatigue.

Many field shooters choose guns which are particularly suited to their favourite form of

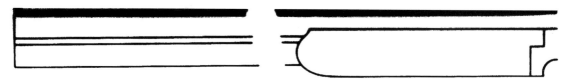

The standard, solid rib is mainly fitted to guns intended for field shooting and is usually ¹/₄in (6mm) wide, and sometimes tapering.

This Winchester 101 Super Grade is one of the best handling game over-and-unders ever sold in the United Kingdom.

The rib of this game gun terminates in a small brass bead foresight, which is quite adequate for the job.

shooting. For instance, a person who shoots a lot of high, driven game from relatively open stances may opt for a slightly heavy gun with barrels up to 30in. The long tubes will help against his relatively distant targets, the weight will help to absorb recoil, and between drives he will carry his gun in its slip, over his shoulder so that the little extra weight is of no consequence. Another shooter who does a lot of walking in dense woodland may need a lighter gun, while barrels as short as 25in will help him to swing rapidly and take relatively fast shots through small gaps among the trees.

These, however, are special requirements, and the average shooter will opt for a 28in gun weighing between 6³/₄ and 7¹/₄lb. That is rather heavier than the classic English side-by-side, but it will shoot comfortably all day and not be too much of a burden for most people. If a lighter gun is required, then a 20-bore weighing 6¹/₂lb or less and firing a ¹³/₁₆oz cartridge is a good alternative. You can even buy a 12-bore which weighs just 6lb, which is fine as long as you stick to light ammunition.

Multichokes are an option on this gun: they make it more adaptable at the expense of only about an ounce of total weight; but that ounce is at the wrong end of the gun and, some feel, may slightly affect perfect balance. Remember that, for the best handling, the main concentration of weight should be in the part of the gun that lies between your hands when you shoot.

Top rib on the game O/U is usually narrow: ¹/₄in (6mm), and sometimes tapering. A small gold or white bead foresight is preferred by most shooters, although a fluorescent bead may be a slight help when shooting at dusk or in darkness. There is no need for a mid-rib bead – mounting usually has to be so fast that you would not have time to take notice of it, even if it were there.

Stock dimensions in terms of the drops at comb and heel will be similar to those in the Sporter, although a good point to remember is that you will be doing most of your game shooting while you are wearing thick winter clothing. For this reason many shooters go for a stock that is anywhere between ¹/₄ and ³/₈in shorter than they require on a competition gun. That is a

This game gun has what is called a semi-pistol grip: a very comfortable option.

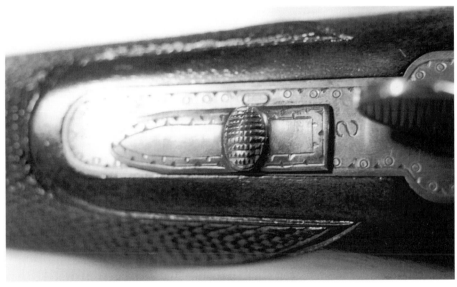

On most single-trigger guns, barrel selection is achieved by moving the safety thumbpiece from side to side. From the exposed 'O' it may be seen that this gun is set to fire top barrel first.

good point to remember if you have a game gun fitted: if the fitting takes place on a summer's day or in a warm room, take your winter gear with you. The gun should be fitted while you are wearing your shooting clothing.

Some O/U game guns are available with straight-hand stocks rather than pistol grips, and some shooters who wish to customize their guns have straight-hand stocks fitted. The real purpose of the traditional straight-hand stock is to allow you to slide your hand back when pulling the back trigger of a double-trigger gun, so why bother to fit one to a gun with a single trigger? The only answer can be elegance, and it has to be admitted that straight-hand stocks on O/U game guns do look elegant. A nice compromise is the gently curving, semi-pistol stock, which gives you the best of both worlds.

Many imported, fixed-choke, game guns are supplied with very tight chokes, a combination

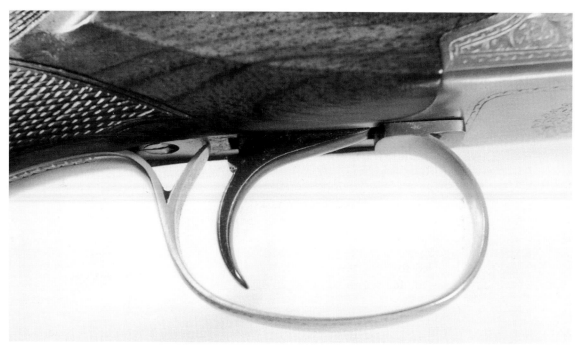

This plain, non-adjustable trigger has a pleasant, smooth curve

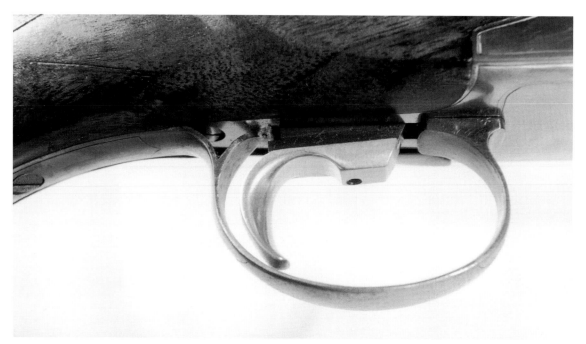

This adjustable trigger slides on a rail and is locked in position by a grub screw, the hole for which may be seen towards the front.

of $1/2$ and full being not uncommon. These are unsuited to most British game shooting except, perhaps, extremely high pheasants and ducks, and most shooters have them opened out a little. A $1/2$ and $1/4$ is a good compromise for most occasions, but a shooter who is constantly faced with relatively close targets may opt for chokes as open as $1/4$ and improved cylinder. Remember that, by and large, many game and general field shooters shoot chokes much tighter than they need, and often pay the penalty for it in terms of missed targets.

For all game and pigeon shooting there is no need to shoot cartridges longer than $2^3/_4$in (70mm), although chambers and proofing to shoot 3in magnum cartridges may be useful if the gun is going to be used for the occasional coastal wildfowling foray, or for certain shoot

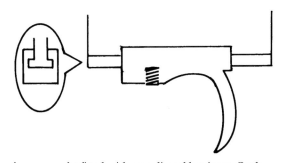

A gun may be fitted with an adjustable trigger. Such triggers usually slide on a 'T'-shaped rail and are locked in position with a single grub screw.

management tasks such as fox control. However, foxes should be tackled only at very close range with a shotgun, and only then in an emergency; a centre-fire rifle is a far better and more humane tool. For 'fowling, the repeated recoil of a 3in magnum through a 7lb gun on the foreshore is going to be punishing. Three-inch chambers are therefore useful to have on occasions, but not strictly necessary. The older English game guns generally have $2^1/2$in (65mm) chambers, and $2^1/_2$in ammunition is quite powerful enough for most game and field shooting tasks.

A game gun should have a barrel selector because it is often desirable to shoot the most

---

The Game Gun Specification

Barrels: 28in (more or less for special purposes), fixed $1/4$ and $1/2$ chokes or multi-chokes; $1/4$in rib with small white bead foresight; chambers $2^3/_4$in or 3in magnum.

Action: boxlock or sidelock; single selective trigger; automatic safety optional.

Stock: pistol or semi-pistol grip; length $14^1/_8$ to $14^3/_8$in; drop at comb $1^1/_2$in, drop at heel $2^1/_2$in; cast to suit shooter.

Fore-end: slim semi-beavertail or schnabel.

Weight: $6^3/_4$ to 7lb for 12-bore; 20-bores may be $1/2$lb lighter.

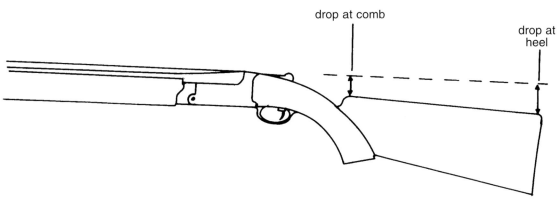

Drops at heel and comb are measured vertically from a line projected back from the line of the rib.

The safety catch on most guns is on the top strap just behind the top lever. It should be knurled like this with a firm grip for a cold thumb.

tightly choked barrel first. An automatic safety, which is applied every time the gun is opened for reloading, is also considered a desirable feature by some shooters, as the normal discipline is to slip off the safety just before you mount the gun to your shoulder. Do remember, however, that an auto safety is no substitute for safe gun-handling discipline.

The Wildfowling Gun

Many inland geese and most ducks are shot with either conventional game guns or sporters. However, coastal wildfowling often calls for slightly longer shots and an ability to shoot the 3in magnum cartridge comfortably is an obvious advantage: it puts more big shot into the pattern and kills at a slightly longer range.

The gun is usually made to almost exactly the same specification as the game gun, with either 28 or 30in barrels fitted with 3in chambers and

subjected to magnum proof. The real difference is in the weight, and unless you are sure that you can bear continued, heavy recoil a gun that weighs between 8 and $8^{1}/_{4}$lb is recommended. It is heavy to carry for long distances, but you will normally carry it to your chosen creek or hide in its slip.

A further important consideration is corrosion resistance, since on the foreshore the guns

---

The Wildfowling Gun Specification

Barrels: 28 or 30in, $^{3}/_{4}$ and full or $^{1}/_{2}$ and $^{3}/_{4}$ fixed choke, or multichoke (follow gun and cartridge manufacturers' recommendations for steel shot); 3in magnum chambers and proofing; superior steel proofing when available.

Weight: 8lb or more.

Other specifications: as game gun.

---

are invariably used in a salt-laden atmosphere and handled with wet, salty hands. A high-quality exterior finish is required, and black-chromed barrels such as are fitted to Spanish-built Lauronas have much to commend them. Varnished stocks, as opposed to the traditional oil finish, may be more resistant to attack on a gun which is going to be constantly used in wet conditions.

The once-common big-bores of 10 and 8 may offer slightly more positive kills at extremes of range, but they are not commonly available in the O/U configuration. There are some side-by-sides available both new and second-hand, but a realistic alternative is a 10-bore semi-auto shooting the American $3^1/_2$in magnum cartridge.

At the time of writing (1997) wildfowlers are being encouraged to use non-toxic, lead-free shot over wetlands and marshes, and such shot may become a legal requirement in the near future. The softer alternatives such as zinc, tin, bismuth and heavy metals incorporated in plastic compounds can all be shot through guns and chokes designed for lead. Light steel loads may also be shot through conventional fixed and multichoke guns, provided that the chokes are not too tight and also provided that the cartridge and gun manufacturers' recommendations are strictly adhered to. Always check both your gun specification and the instructions on the cartridge packet before firing them. Multi-choke tubes provided with new game and 'fowling guns are usually marked with recommendations for steel.

Heavy steel loads should not be shot through any guns currently available on the British market, although, within a few years guns bearing a superior steel proof should be available. More information on this point may be found in Chapter 11.

3 MAKING YOUR GUN FIT YOU

No matter how much you pay, standard, over-the-counter shotguns do not suit everyone. Their dimensions are tailored to fit a Mr Average who, as far as I can work out, is between 5ft 8in and 5ft 10in tall, not too wide across the shoulders, weighs between 12 and 13 stone, and is right-handed.

This is not a lot of help if you are taller or shorter, very plump or very thin, a woman, have long or short arms compared to your body size, are left-handed, have a short or a long neck, or have some permanent injury or disability to your upper body. In deference to the gun trade, many guns are available with left-handed stocks, but all other situations are going to call for some modification if you are to shoot well and comfortably. You may also feel that there is some improvement which could be made to the gun's balance to make it perform better.

TAKE ADVICE

Books have been written about gun fitting, and I am still not convinced that even the best can offer more than general guidelines and advice. You will learn more from a skilled coach or fitter in five minutes than you will if you study a book for a month; and so, if you feel that you have a problem, get down to your local shooting ground or gun shop and seek professional advice. In terms of cash investment, it will be the best money you ever spend on your shooting. Don't listen to friends unless they are very skilled – you will be wasting your time. And don't just soldier on with the thought that you will get better the more you get used to the gun. If it is forcing you to shoot in an undesirable position you never will improve, although you will waste a fortune on ammunition and targets. It is far better to seek what at first appears to be the most expensive option and go to a good professional.

A good fitter or coach will give you an ideal 'recipe' for a gun that is tailored to your particular physical frame. Armed with that specification you can then take your gun to a gunsmith and ask him to get on with it, or you can try a few things yourself to see what the improvement is likely to be. We can call these non-permanent modifications.

STOCKTAKING

For instance, if a stock is too short the gun may hurt you on recoil, and in an extreme case you may be in danger of giving yourself a hard bang on the nose with the thumb that is hooked over the hand of the stock. You are also not going to get a correct sight picture and you may shoot high. A temporary measure is to buy an object that looks like a rubber or lace-up leather boot from your gun shop and slip it over the foot of the stock. In order to work properly it must be tightly fitting, and it may be a bit 'snaggy' on your clothing when you mount the gun, but it will get you going until you can have a permanent modification made. In other words, try it but do not use it permanently unless it really does the trick and is very comfortable.

The fitting of a thick recoil pad may offer a permanent solution, but some of these pads may be rather 'sticky' and are best suited only for trap guns. An alternative is to get a thick buttplate made from vulcanite or some other

If you use black vulcanite to extend a stock much longer than this the results may be rather ugly. It is better to make the extension of well-matched wood.

This simple buttplate is excellent – hard and with just the right profile for slick mounting.

hard, black, impact-resistant plastic; but these items may look very ugly if they are more than about ³/₄in thick. They leave a thick, black 'stripe' at the back of the gun which makes it look tail-heavy and out of balance, even if it is not. For a longer extension it is better to get a gunsmith to find an offcut of walnut with a grain that matches that of your stock as nearly as possible. It is even possible for a skilled man to draw on a matching representation of the grain with black ink. Whatever you do, remember that all extensions must be extremely firmly fitted and

allow access to the gun's stock-retaining bolt. You will also need a new buttplate, because the old one will be too short for the extended stock if an elegant profile is to be retained.

If a stock is too long there is no quick modification: you will just have to get it shortened. You may feel competent to saw the wood off yourself, but do remember that the job must be done neatly if the gun is to retain its resale value. Also remember that the buttplate will have to be reprofiled or it will overhang at the bottom, and possibly at the top and the sides

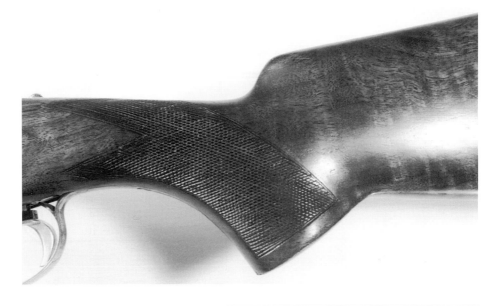

The curve on this pistol-grip stock is very comfortable, while the general dimensions would suit a sporter or a skeet gun.

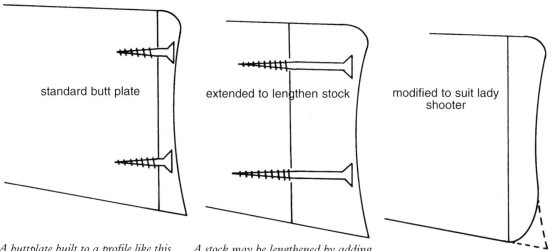

A buttplate built to a profile like this suits most people for field shooting, sporting clays and skeet. The slightly rounded heel often helps with a speedy mount, preventing the butt from snagging on clothing.

A stock may be lengthened by adding a longer buttplate made of hard, black vulcanite, although a long extension made of this material looks ugly and is best made of a wood carefully matched to the grain and colour of the stock.

Many women shooters find it more comfortable to shoot with a buttplate of this profile, with the toe rounded off.

too. For a gun that has to be significantly shortened for a youngster it is common to save the sawn-off piece of wood so that it may be put back in a few years' time. When considering this work beware of the fact that some semi-auto stocks can only be shortened by half an inch or less, because the bolt return spring runs through the stock centre. If you are short in stature this could affect your choice of semi-auto in the first place.

If the comb of the stock is too low or too slim its profile can be temporarily altered by sticking strips of card to it with masking tape. This is a good trick if you are fitting your own stock because you can build it up gradually in small increments until you get it right. And, once you have it right, there is still no need to have the modification made permanent: you can replace the card with the same thickness of leather,

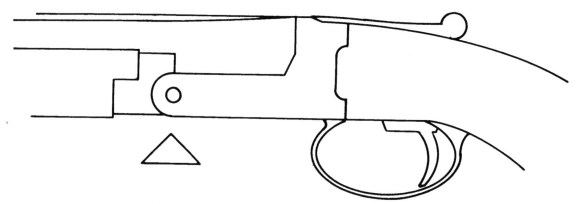

For fast handling, a gun should balance on the hinge pin, although many modern O/Us balance 3/8in (10mm) further forward. A balance point significantly further forward than that causes the gun to feel nose-heavy and slow-handling.

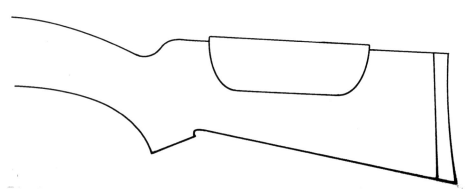

The comb of a gun may be raised by sticking on a cheek piece made of leather. Comb-raising kits, working on this principle, are available from many gun shops.

stuck on with a rubber-based adhesive. Old leather handbags, bought cheaply from charity shops, are a good source of material, or you can get your gun shop to find for you a comb-raising kit which will do the same job with precut pieces of leather or fabric.

Like the stock that is too long, the only cure for a comb that is too high is to take it to a gun-smith and have it shaved down or bent. The bending is a tricky job which involves heating the wood in the hand of the stock with hot oil until it becomes plastic and then clamping it in position with the right bend until it cools and sets. It is generally a job for the professionals and, even then, it is not always permanent. Some samples of walnut bend more readily than others, while a few will not bend at all, and some tend to creep back to their original profile in a matter of months or even weeks. The answer in these cases is to have a stocker recut the fit between the head of the stock and the action. There are also a few guns made with a metal sleeve through the stock bolt hole, and these stocks cannot be bent at all.

CAST

Cast is the amount of deviation between the centre line of the barrels and the centre line of the stock in the horizontal plane – the 'sideways' bend of the stock. This can also show itself as an apparent twist if the amounts of cast at the heel

and the toe are different. Most standard stocks have a cast of between an $1/8$ and $1/4$in at the heel with – frequently – more cast at the toe. This bend and twist places the buttplate slightly to the right for a right-handed shooter and slightly to the left for a left-hander, and its purpose is to put the centre line of the rib directly in front of your eye when the stock is mounted comfortably in your shoulder pocket. It therefore follows that those with wide shoulders generally require more cast than those of slimmer build. Right-handed stocks can be bent to suit left-handers, and vice versa, but the usual limit of bend is around $3/4$in and not with all stocks; if you require more than that an expensive, specially made stock is the only way to go. However, the normal limits of bend accommodate nearly everyone and left-handed stocks are often available from importers.

WOMEN ARE SHOOTERS TOO

With most guns being made to fit Mr Average, women often seem to be forgotten. They naturally have their own special requirements – largely because they are generally shorter in stature, less physically strong and finer boned than men. They also tend to have longer necks and hollower cheeks. These physical characteristics often call for quite drastic stock alterations. Combs sometimes need to be raised, occasionally to the point that Sporter, game gun and skeet stocks are best replaced with trap stocks. Women also often require the woodwork to be thickened in the comb to compensate for their slimmer cheeks; while great care has to be taken with the dimensions of the woodwork in the hand so that shorter, slimmer fingers can comfortably reach the trigger.

Women are also generally more recoil-sensitive than men, and it is not always just because they have lighter, slimmer features. It is because the buttplate of the average gun is the wrong shape for them. Immediately below the shoulder pocket most men have a relatively strong pectoral muscle which is able to absorb the recoil through the toe of the stock without discomfort or bruising. On women this area consists of softer, easily bruised tissue, and the answer is usually to round off the extreme toe of the stock so that it does not make contact there. Recoil pain in this region often causes female newcomers to mount the stock either outwards towards the point of the shoulder or too high, causing further pain and discomfort as well as missed targets, so it is an important point to heed. When teaching a woman to shoot, the normal instruction is to mount the buttplate on her bra strap, and this usually ensures that it finishes up in the right place.

Another point for women shooters to watch is that of gun weight. Most women, when they first pick up a gun, complain that it is heavy when, in fact, its weight may be well within their physical capabilities after a little training. The temptation is to provide them with a very light gun which, unless fed with pipsqueak cartridges, is going to hurt them with recoil. In shooting there is no valid reason why women should not compete on level terms with men and the concept of 'a little gun for the girls' is not something many women would wish to encourage and neither is it necessary. Some of our women champions are very slightly built indeed, yet they shoot full-weight guns and normal competition ammunition, so all the possibilities of fitting and balance should be explored before gun weight is significantly reduced.

BALANCE

Balance is another important aspect of good gun handling and, although there are individual preferences, the consensus is that the balance point should be either on the hinge pin or no more than half an inch in front of it. Most guns are constructed to this ideal, but sometimes things go slightly awry. One of the main culprits in poor balance is the wide variance of density in different samples of stock wood. Very dense walnut, usually but not always dark in colour, may be as much as 4oz heavier than less dense material. Good advice to anyone buying a new gun is first to choose the make and model, then – if there is a choice – pick the one with the heaviest woodwork because additional weight at the back end of the stock can slightly slow down the gun's handling.

A dense stock may be lightened by careful

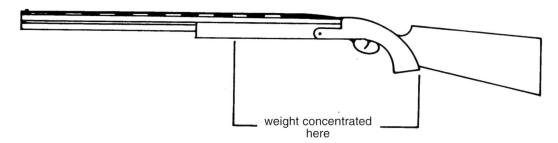

weight concentrated here

For ideal handling, the main weight of a gun should be concentrated in the area between the hands when it is held in the shooting position. Significant weight outside this area makes handling feel ponderous.

When considering ribs and sights, remember that a shotgun is pointed and not brought to deliberate aim like this Browning rifle.

hollowing, usually by boring out the stock bolt hole by as much as is safe and cutting it to an elliptical cross-section rather than a round one. However, this is rarely necessary, but light stocks often require more weight to be added in order to restore balance. The trick is to be able to do it without permanently blocking the stock bolt hole, as, sooner or later in any gun's life, the stock will have to come off and neither the owner nor his gunsmith should have to subject it first to major and possibly damaging surgery.

One method is to cut a thin washer of sheet lead to the exact size of the buttplate and place it underneath the plate as a sandwich. On one gun, which needed to be lengthened by $1/4$in as well as significantly weighted, I fashioned the plate from $1/4$in sheet brass and killed both birds with one stone. Another successful method is to fill the stock bolt hole almost to the top with a slice cut from a thick sheet of relatively hard polystyrene, then sandwich a small sea-fishing weight under the buttplate. The important point is that the weight must neither move nor be shaken loose under recoil; but, if you get the dimensions of the polystyrene plug just right and wrap the weight in tape until it fits snugly, the weight may be removed easily once the buttplate has been taken off and the plug itself removed with a corkscrew. A further alternative is to fashion a lead weight that just fits the stock bolt hole and attach it to the buttplate with a countersunk bolt passed through from the back. If the weight required is small a further alternative, passed on to me by a *Sporting Gun* reader, is to use a piece of a self-adhesive car-wheel weight stuck to the underside of the buttplate in a place where it coincides with the stock bolt hole. These are the weights used to stick on alloy wheels, so that the contact between different metals does not cause electrolytic corrosion.

Some shooters require a little weight to be added at the muzzles, usually to slow down an over-lively gun. The only neat way of doing this, to the best of my knowledge, is to machine or file small steel weights of half-moon section and about a couple of inches long and attach them to the gun's side ribs with small screws running into drilled and tapped holes. If the weights are well finished and blacked it is hardly possible to see them.

ONCE MORE – TAKE ADVICE

In one way and another there is much you can do to make your gun more comfortable to shoot, and many of the modifications are quite cheap. Don't let anyone persuade you that you will learn to adapt to a gun that is an appalling fit – you never will completely and, along the way, you may pick up some bad habits that could stay with you for the rest of your shooting life. You would not put up with a chair that gave you a pain in the back, so why put up with a gun that gives you a pain in the neck? Do yourself a favour, get expert advice from a fitter or coach and then get it altered.

4 CHECKING A USED GUN

EARLY DAYS

I am old enough to have shot when a gun licence cost six shillings (30p) over the Post Office counter and there was no police examination in order to get one. My first licence was bought from old Mrs Clarke, the postmistress in our small town, and she told me to be careful and not mix with 'those rough lads who went down the marshes in winter'. I ignored her advice about undesirable company – and thus enjoyed myself hugely and started to gain a working knowledge of the countryside.

We lads bought extremely cheap guns, even acquired them as swaps for bicycles, fishing rods, ferrets and other sundry items of property which were vital to the normal life of youngsters in a small Lincolnshire town in the 1950s. And most of those guns were horrible: loose and rattly, with pitted tubes, cracked woodwork and almost every mechanical fault you could imagine. A gun that was thought to be 'a bit dodgy' was subjected to our simple safety check: it was loaded with an Eley Alphamax cartridge – the most powerful commonly available – tied to a fence post and fired with a long piece of string attached to the trigger. If it survived it was a good 'un.

How we managed not to blow ourselves up I shall never know, and the fact that we did not says much for the reserves of strength built into most guns. But it is strength never to be taken for granted and, if I were now asked to fire the gun I had when I was seventeen, I would refuse on the grounds of safety. Buying and shooting guns of dubious reliability is a mug's game fraught with danger both for the shooter and the onlookers and therefore for the reputation of the shooting sports.

THE PROOF HOUSE MARK

Added to this there are some popular myths about the safety of guns. Many still believe that if a gun has a proof house stamp on the barrel and the words 'Nitro Proof' then it is safe. This is not necessarily so: all that the Proof House mark means is that the gun was safe with the cartridge for which it was designed to be used on the day that it was tested. That day could have been fifty or more years ago, and since then the gun could have fired many thousands of cartridges and have been subjected to all kinds of misuse as well as general wear and tear. The firing of just one over-powered or over-length cartridge could have rendered it unsafe on the day after it was bought. It could also have been repaired in an unsafe, amateurish manner.

It is a criminal offence to sell a gun that is out of proof, and the law applies equally to individual shooters as well as professionals in the trade. The difference is that a registered firearms dealer has his reputation to protect and it is in his interest to ensure that every gun he sells both conforms with the law and satisfies his client. He should also have the knowledge, and the instruments, to make the necessary checks to ensure that the proof marks are still valid. An individual gun owner may consider himself not to be bound by any such constraints, but he should remember that, as in all things, ignorance of the law is no excuse. All this boils down to is the fact that every gun offered under private sale should be examined by a professional gunsmith before the deal is finalized. The gunsmith will make a small charge, but it is money well invested and an honest seller should welcome this safeguard.

Most gun shops have a good selection on the second-hand rack, but care must be taken in sorting the good from the mediocre.

CHECKING FOR YOURSELF

That said, there are many checks to which you can subject a gun offered in private sale before you get to the gunsmith's door. The first is nothing more than a cursory examination of the exterior. If the gun looks old and battered then that is what it is, and if the owner has failed to lavish care on the outside, why should the inner workings be any different? A gun covered in dents, scratches and rust flecks on the outside probably has rusty workings inside, and possibly rust too in places that you will never be able to see, such as under the ribs. This may sound obvious, but many a gun described by its owner as 'a tough old faithful that has never let me down in

twenty years' is nothing more than a rusty rattletrap that is well overdue for major gunsmithing attention or even the scrapheap.

Now I shall run through the checks I normally perform on the second-hand test guns I write about in *Sporting Gun*. In order to be methodical, I usually start at the front end and work towards the back, hoping that thereby I miss nothing.

THE BARRELS

Is the blacking worn, and if so, why? It may be that the gun is just old and much-handled, but patches of bright metal may indicate that it has been left uncovered in a car boot for a long journey and allowed to rub against some abrasive object. Blotchy blacking, with thin patches and some a different shade from others, often indicates an inexpert repair with blacking compounds bought over a gunsmith's counter. Expect to find small rub-marks under the fore-end wood of most O/Us; but they should not be more than surface marks and there certainly should not be scratches that go beyond the blacking. Deep scratches elsewhere on the barrels are also suspicious, and rust anywhere is bad news. Look for it particularly carefully in the nooks and crannies such as the slots in side ribs and under the bridges in the top rib. Do not be alarmed if, when apparently spotless and well blacked barrels are wiped with a lightly oiled cloth, the cloth comes away with a very slight, brown, rusty-looking tinge. That is normal.

Multichoke tubes, if they are present, should screw in and out easily and the threads should be slightly greasy. Try all the available tubes in the gun and, if you find one that is stiff to turn and the thread is clean, bear in mind that it could have been dropped or trodden on and may be slightly distorted. Enough distortion to render the tube out of round may not be visible to the human eye, but tightness in the thread may be a clue. Any multichoke tube damaged in any way needs to be replaced, because it cannot be safely repaired.

This part of a gun, that which retains the fore-end, is called the fore-end loop.

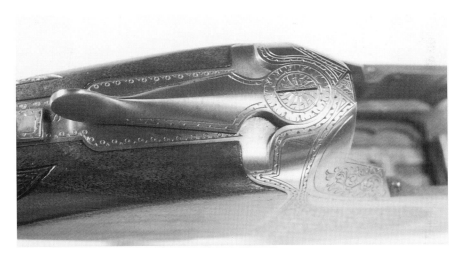

Slots in all the screw heads on a gun should point fore-and-aft, like the one in the screw which secures this top lever. If they do not, it may be a sign of amateur or botched gunsmithing.

Moving backwards, the rib on an O/U should be straight and true, without dents. Some O/U ribs are very thin and, standing up on bridges as they do, are easily bent and dented when in contact with tree branches or the top rails of cages used in the sporting disciplines. If dents have been removed expertly you should not be able to see where they were. If a small dent is present, look underneath it to see that there is no corresponding small dent in the top of the barrel, caused by somebody trying to lift the rib dent with a screwdriver. Rib dents need to be lifted carefully with specialist tools.

The classic method of checking a set of barrels for loose ribs and other possible evils is to suspend them by the barrel lumps and give them a sharp tap with a pencil or a thumbnail. The sound, it is said, should be a clear ring, like a bell. In fact, I have found that many completely sound O/U barrel sets, particularly those made on the monobloc principle, often respond to this treatment with a rather dull thud, so the test is not completely reliable. However, any slight rattle accompanying whatever sound you hear may indicate a rib that needs expert attention. Loose ribs are more common on English side-by-sides which have been assembled with soft solder; but they may also happen on more modern guns held together by harder and more durable brazing alloys.

Listen, also, for little 'trundling' noises when the barrels are tipped from the horizontal. These

This typical ventilated top rib is rather thin in section and could be easily damaged by a sharp blow.

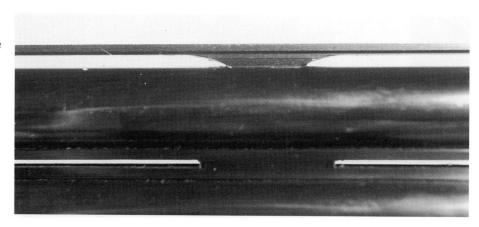

could indicate loose material – often blobs of solder – underneath the solid side ribs on an O/U or the top rib on a side-by-side. Usually these sounds are annoying rather than indicative of damage, but they may indicate that a rib has been resoldered at some time.

Next, examine the barrel lumps. Deep scores may indicate that the gun has been closed on a grain of sharp grit or that it has been opened and closed when completely dry of lubrication and the metal surfaces have 'picked up' on each other. Dents such as deep punch marks around the hook of a gun with a full-width hinge pin or around the semi-circular cut-outs of a gun which hinges on stub pins may indicate an amateur attempt to tighten a loose action, as may similar marks on the fore-end loop. While in this area, examine the proof marks. Some guide lines as to what you should find and details of acceptable foreign proof marks are contained in the excellent booklet *Notes on the Proof of Shotguns and Other Small Arms*, available for a small charge from the Birmingham and the London Proof Houses.

While in this area, look at the ejectors. Non-spring-loaded components should slide freely in their tracks without any feeling of 'grittiness', and you should be able to press in spring-loaded ejectors with your thumb, using some force and taking care not to cut yourself on sharp edges, and they should spring back smoothly. Both types should be very lightly oiled, without dirt or rust underneath. Next try to see whether the ejectors have splayed outwards slightly with long use, because if they have they may override the heads of some cartridge cases, leaving you with an empty case stuck in the barrel. If ejectors have become splayed the safest repair is replacement, but those on discontinued guns for which there are no spares may sometimes be straightened by a gunsmith. However, there is always a risk of breakage.

Inside, the barrel tubes should be bright and shiny. Pitting shows up as black or dark grey marks, and the beginnings of pitting may appear as a dull grey etch mark on the surface. A gun with internally chromed bores that looks greyish towards the muzzles may have had over-tight chokes opened out by a gunsmith, the dullness being where the chrome has been ground away, leaving plain steel underneath. If this is so, any reamer marks should have been polished out. Bulges generally show as dark rings, while dents distort straight lines of reflected light. They can often be spotted if you look through the barrel when it is held pointed towards the edge of a window frame. Try to look at the barrel walls rather than through the tubes, and, unless you are a skilled bulge and dent spotter, do not necessarily trust your own judgement. The finding of such defects calls for a trained eye and is really a job for a gunsmith. If you do spot what appears to be a dent on the inside there is often a small corresponding mark on the outside blacking.

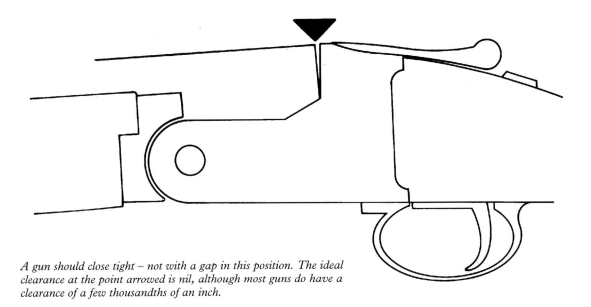

A gun should close tight – not with a gap in this position. The ideal clearance at the point arrowed is nil, although most guns do have a clearance of a few thousandths of an inch.

THE JOINTING

This is the vital hinge mechanism of the gun, and undue looseness in it may render the gun out of proof. The first check is to assemble the gun without the fore-end and, if spring-loaded ejectors are fitted, to take them out before assembling the gun if you are able to, because they may press back against the standing breech and give a false impression of tightness. Then clamp the stock under your arm and try to move the barrels against the action, both up and down and from side to side. You should be able to detect no movement at all. In fact, the ideal clearance between the barrel breech ends and the standing breech is absolutely nil. In practice, many guns have a gap about the thickness of a sheet of aluminium foil, but if the gap fails to trap a sheet of ordinary writing paper, then an expert opinion is required.

Next, fit the fore-end and check it for tightness; there should be no detectable movement either fore and aft or from side to side. If any previously noticed looseness seems to disappear when the fore-end is fitted the gun is still not safe, and loose jointing may have been tightened by forcing the fore-end iron back on to the knuckles. If there is a movement in the fore-end

itself, make sure that it is not just loose wood – which can often be rectified by tightening the attachment screws. These screws are particularly prone to shooting loose on some guns and may be secured with a smear of soft-setting Loctite.

The gun should open fully to allow cartridges to be loaded, and should stay fully open until you close it. If, to open the gun fully, you feel that you are having to force it against a spring and, when fully opened, it springs part of the way back, then there could be a problem with the cocking rods or the sears. Again, you will need an expert opinion.

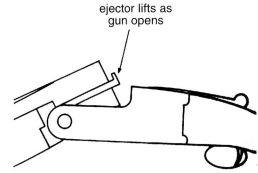

ejector lifts as
gun opens

The ejectors on a used gun should work smoothly and should eject fired cases simultaneously from both barrels. This can be checked by using snap caps.

THE ACTION

The action should be clean, rust-free and without scratches on the outside and, if it is plated, the plating should be free from blemishes which might indicate that water has got underneath. Bright patches on a blackened or colour-hardened action, trigger guard or top lever are general indicators of a lot of use. The part of the action that you can see inside should be clean and very lightly oiled. Any gun that has been fired fairly frequently is going to have circular marks corresponding to the cartridge heads on the standing breech, but these should be surface marks only and not indentations.

Also look at any exposed screw heads on the outside of the action. When a gun is made it is usual to fit screws so that the slots in their heads lie exactly parallel with the barrel bores, and good gunsmiths always replace screws with a similar alignment. Screw slots that lie at angles may be an indication of amateurish repair, as may screw slots with burrs or chips caused by the use of unsuitable screwdrivers.

The top lever should lie either parallel with the rib or with the tip just to the right of it when viewed from the rear. A top lever that lies slightly the other way may indicate a worn bolting mechanism, and any free movement in the top lever is very bad news. When you push the top lever over it should give the impression of being held by a firm but pliant spring. A slightly 'floppy' feeling may indicate a coil spring that is so old and tired that it is no longer of its original length. I have seen top lever springs which, when removed, were a quarter of an inch shorter than a new component, but their replacement is relatively cheap.

Next look down the firing pin holes, using a magnifying glass unless you have perfect eyesight. The tips of the pins should be rounded, without chips and without cratering. Cratered tips are particularly common in Winchesters and Mirokus and, unless the affected components are replaced, a flake will eventually break off the side of the pin tip and leave you with an inoperable gun. When the gun is opened the bottom firing pin of an O/U should always be fully retracted down its hole by spring pressure. Some guns have free-floating top pins which can slide forward when the gun is tilted downwards.

You can check the trigger or triggers by load-

A full-width hinge pin such as this can, if necessary, be withdrawn and replaced with one of slightly greater diameter to compensate for wear in the gun's jointing.

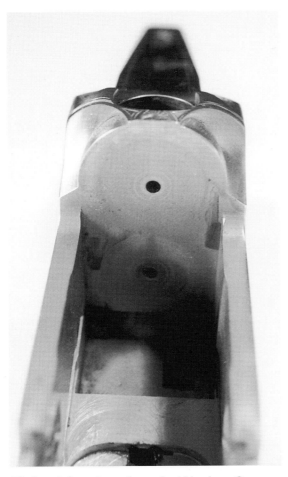

The breech face of a used gun should be clean. Some circular marks concentric with the firing pin holes are inevitable, but they should have no depth.

Even when buying a new gun, such as one of the Berettas in the foreground, a gun shop which allows the opportunity of firing before purchase offers a great advantage.

ing the gun with snap caps. Dry-firing the gun without them may lead to damage, so don't do it. Triggers should fire with a pull of approximately 4lb or slightly less, and very light pulls are dangerous. There should be scarcely any detectable movement on the trigger when the lock fires, although the triggers of cheap guns are often a bit 'creepy' and no amount of regulation will make them perfect. The ideal trigger feels like an icicle snapping when the lock fires.

If the gun has a single trigger and switches to

its second barrel with a mechanism driven by the recoil of the cartridge in the first barrel going off, nothing is going to happen when you pull the trigger for the second time. To reset this type of mechanism when using snap caps, give the butt a sharp tap against a carpeted floor or the toe of your boot. Checking this kind of mechanism by moving the barrel selector between 'shots' is no indication that it is working properly; the transfer mechanism could be gummed up with old oil, set so that it will operate only with ammunition more powerful than that you will want to use, or even not operate at all.

When you open a gun which is an ejector, both snap caps should fly out together, not one after the other. This is called good ejector timing and, although it is not vital to the operation of the gun, the lack of it could indicate general wear or that a fault in one ejector is not many shots away.

After this you can fire each barrel singly, but with both barrels loaded with snap caps. When you open the gun only the cap from the fired barrel should be ejected. If both caps fly out there is a fault, usually caused by a jammed or bent ejector rod.

Before you look further, check that the safety and the barrel selector – if there is one – actually work. The safety should have a positive to-and-fro movement without a 'gritty' feel, and when it is applied the trigger should feel as if it is positively blocked or disengaged. It is not unknown for a worn or badly regulated safety to allow the trigger to fire with the application of about twice the normal pressure, so do check. The barrel selector should work smoothly, and most of the type which are incorporated in the safety thumbpiece can be moved only when the safety is in the 'safe' position.

You may find other types: sometimes there is a cross-button either in the trigger root or close to the trigger and occasionally – notably on some Baikal models – the gun is set to fire top barrel first by pushing the trigger forward until it clicks.

If you have the tools, and the owner's permission, you may then remove the stock and look inside the mechanism. It should be clean, free from rust and only just damp with fine oil. A gummy mechanism, frequently accompanied by a smell of soluble oil, usually indicates that a gun has been carelessly cleaned with a solvent designed to be diluted in water. The solution has been allowed to run back through the firing pin holes and go semi-solid in the mechanism as the water has dried out. I have known this stuff to cause inertia-type barrel selectors to seize up completely, added to which it may promote the formation of rust. The presence of a lot of lubri-cating oil may indicate that important parts of the stock have been soaked in oil and softened. We shall look at that later.

THE WOODWORK

Any gun that has had a fair amount of use will have small scars and dents on the woodwork, but they should not be deep. What you are really looking for at this stage are cracks, because they always spell trouble and may be indicators of much worse damage than appears on the surface. I once investigated a microscopic surface crack in the head of a stock, just behind the gun's top strap, and discovered that it was the one visible sign of a stock that was totally wrecked inside – so really do look closely.

Start with the fore-end and pay particular attention to the area around the latch, and where the wood meets the metal of the fore-end iron at the back. The corners of sharp angles in this area are particularly prone to damage, especially on some guns where the wood is very thin. If you do see a crack follow it right through to the inside of the wood, where it may be worse than on the surface.

The most important area of the stock is its head, because that is where all the recoil forces are concentrated when the gun is fired. Particularly critical areas are at the back of the top strap and the corresponding area at the bottom, behind the trigger guard. Cracks found in these areas must be investigated particularly thoroughly, and for a proper examination you must remove the stock. The grain through the hand of a stock should run fore-and-aft and follow the curve as much as possible, not diagonally nor crossways. Some very pretty stocks may be a bit cross-grained in this area, but they are potentially weak and often cannot be bent if alterations are required to make the gun fit.

Another critical area is the toe of the stock, and a crack there often indicates that a gun has been dropped sharply. Also look on the area of the outside of the stock which is level with the position of the stock bolt head inside. A crack here may indicate that at some stage a large screwdriver has slipped off the bolt head and gouged the wood.

Some small cracks may be glued and pinned, while others cannot. The purchase of a gun with a crack of any sort should always be the subject of expert opinion, because a new stock often costs more than the value of the gun. This applies particularly to guns which have been out of production for a long time and for which spare woodwork has to be handmade. Such repairs cost a great deal of money, some to the point where it may be cheaper to scrap the gun and buy another.

Next, carefully examine every area where wood meets metal and make sure that there are no gaps. Gaps between wood and metal at the head often indicate that a new stock has been inexpertly fitted and, if this is the case, cracking in the near future is a distinct possibility. The forces of recoil must be evenly distributed through the wood, and not applied to localized contact points. Beware of the old trick of filling wood-to-metal gaps with brown boot polish.

Staining with mineral oil is another point to watch for in these wood-to-metal areas. In the head of a stock it often indicates that the gun has been stored upright with too much oil in the barrels and that this has run down, through the firing pin holes and into the action and from there into the wood. If this has happened, the wood inside may be dangerously soft so, again, an internal examination is called for. Woodwork can also be killed by kindness, and the application of too much linseed or proprietary stock oil may have the same softening effect. On a gun that has been quickly smartened up for sale fresh stock oil may still be tacky to the touch.

Next look at the chequering. A gun claimed to be 'nearly new' should have diamonds with sharp, crisply defined tips. These tips wear off with constant handling, and the lines between the diamonds become filled in with a mixture of perspiration and dust. Such dirt can be removed with a stiff-bristled brush and its absence on an old gun can be indicative of a high standard of care.

In general, woodwork faults are usually more important than minor mechanical deficiencies. Triggers can be regulated and 'tired' springs replaced relatively cheaply, while even complete rejointing is often not too expensive, but woodwork faults are often very costly to put right.

GENERAL POINTS

Always check the serial number of a used gun, and make sure that the same number is stamped on the fore-end, the barrels and the action. If the numbers are different the gun could have been assembled from a collection of spare parts. This does not necessarily indicate danger if the work has been well done, but such a gun should bear the marks of re-proofing, because the rules demand that all the major components should be proofed together. The enlargement of fixed chokes does not require a re-proofing, but the removal of metal from further back down the barrel tubes – for instance, barrel porting or the lengthening of forcing cones – does. The fitting of multichokes to a gun which was manufactured as a fixed-choke also warrants a visit to a proof house.

There are also other mechanical processes which may render apparently sound guns dangerous. All operations involving the application of much heat to stress-bearing components are potentially dangerous because the steel may lose its hardness. The presence of brazing spelter or silver solder on the surface of a component may indicate such a repair.

Do bear in mind that if you have any of the work described above done to your own gun you do not have to have it re-proofed, although it is always a wise precaution for your own safety and peace of mind. The Proof Regulations are concerned with public safety, and come into operation only when guns are sold. If you choose to blow yourself up, then that's your business, but do be aware that cheap, amateurish repairs usually work out to be the most expensive in the long run.

THE LEGAL SIDE

Make sure that any person from whom you are buying a gun has a valid shotgun certificate and that the gun for sale is listed on that certificate.

Currently (1997) you may possess as many shotguns as you wish on a single certificate, but the firearms office of the relevant police force must be informed of every transaction and each one must be recorded in the relevant sections of both the buyer's and the seller's certificate. Make sure that this is done properly and, if you are confused, the firearms department at your area police headquarters will be pleased to help and will not mind a telephone call. When you buy a gun, write to your police firearms office that day and tell them exactly what you have bought, then you will not forget. Most will also accept this information by fax, if you find that more convenient.

If you wish to try out a gun and the seller is in agreement, you could in 1997 legally borrow it for a period of up to 72 hours without informing the police, but it must be returned or a transaction completed before that period expires.

Note that this is only a brief résumé of the laws which apply to England, Scotland and Wales. Northern Ireland has its own separate shotgun legislation, and the Royal Ulster Constabulary will tell you how it works. The same goes for the Irish Republic – speak to the Garda.

SEMI-AUTOMATICS AND PUMP ACTIONS

The general rules for checking used break-action shotguns also apply to semi-autos and pump actions although, obviously, there is no hinge mechanism to check. Particular points on very old guns include the examination of the receiver for fatigue cracks, particularly behind the bolt handle slot, and the checking for worn guide rails inside. On some guns, notably Remingtons, these rails wear to a razor-sharp profile, so watch your fingers!

Also check that semi-autos will fire your pre-ferred cartridges. Some older guns were built to cycle $1^1/_8$oz (32g) cartridges and fail to work, or work erratically, with anything lighter. Some gas-fed guns can be modified (usually by enlarging the gas ports), but the old, long-recoil Browning Auto 5 is particularly sticky in this respect and much prefers cartridges with $1^1/_8$oz or more of shot.

To be held on a shotgun certificate, all magazine-type shotguns must have fixed rather than removable magazines, and the magazines must not be capable of holding more than two cartridges. In other words, they must be no more than three-shot guns: two in the magazine and one in the chamber. All magazine guns which were originally manufactured with a greater capacity and have since had that capacity reduced by modification must have the modification approved by a proof house. The indication is a tiny stamp (crossed swords for Birmingham and a scimitar for London), incorporating the year of approval and the letters MR (Birmingham) or RM (London). On pumps and semi-autos these marks are usually stamped on the underside of the receiver, just behind the magazine tube.

Many of these modified guns were also issued with a proof house certificate at the time of checking, but many of these certificates have been lost. Police forces no longer insist that they should be produced, as long as the stamps are in order.

Note that these magazine regulations refer to all repeating actions and not just semi-autos and pumps with tubular magazines. There are a few bolt-action guns around with removable, box magazines, and these magazines have to be fixed in place in such a way that they cannot be removed.

DATING SECOND-HAND GUNS

Wouldn't life be easier if the year of manufacture were clearly stamped on all shotguns? On the second-hand market we would know exactly what we were buying, and we would even know whether a 'new' gun had been hanging about on the dealer's rack for years.

As things stand, both the manufacturers and the proof authorities seem to delight in setting puzzles, and in order to date most modern O/Us and semi-autos you have to be a mixture of detective, cryptologist and gun-trade archivist. However, quite precise dating is often possible if you are able to follow the clues. For instance, all modern Brownings and Mirokus have a date code in the serial number. Every number has two letters on the end, and Z = 1, Y = 2, X = 3, W = 4, V = 5, T = 6, R = 7, P = 8, N = 9 and M = 0. Thus a gun with a serial number ending PN was made in 1989. Simple and logical, when you know the code.

The Italians do things differently and, since 1954, have built a date code into their proof marks. To understand the markings from 1954 to 1974 you have to be able to read Roman numerals: 1954 was X (10) and 1974 was XXX (30). Thus a gun marked XXI (21) went through the proof house at Gardone Val Trompia in 1965. To do things the easy way, work out the Roman numerals and then add 44.

With their love of mysteries and secret codes, the Italians changed the system at the end of 1974, and adopted a letter code. That would be easily cracked if the Italian alphabet had used the full set of twenty-six letters and had the national proof authorities not also decided to miss out additional ones for no apparent reason. This being the case, the easiest thing is for me to list the codes: AA = 1975, AB = 1976, AC = 1977, AD = 1978, AE = 1979, AF = 1980, AH = 1981, AI = 1982, AL = 1983, AM = 1984, AN = 1985; AP = 1986; AS = 1987, AT = 1988; AU = 1989, AZ = 1990, BA = 1991, BB = 1992, BC = 1993, BD = 1994, BF = 1995 and BH = 1996.

This date code applies to all guns proofed in Italy: Berettas, Perazzis, Fabarms, the modern series of Classic Doubles, Lincolns, Bettinsolis, Rizzinis and Benellis, to name the common ones. If you wonder where your gun was proofed, the Italian mark is a five-pointed star inside a toothed circle like a gear wheel, with the letters PSF underneath. Two stars on the top of

PSF mean magnum proof and with all guns there is also usually a similar star on top of the word FINITO.

Unfortunately, the Spanish proof masters at Eibar apply no such twisted logic, although importers generally keep good records and can generally trace a gun through its serial number. Lanbers may be approximately dated in this way without the need to question the importers, Gunmark: 130000 = 1977, 155000 = 1978, 190000 = 1982, 226000 = 1985, 267000 = 1987, 305000 = 1990, 310000 = 1991, 320000 = 1992, 330000 = 1993, 340000 = 1994, 350000 = 1995 and 360000 = 1996.

In the USA, where there is no gun-barrel proof legislation, they are not as logical with numbers as you might expect. Winchester never published a list of serial numbers by date for their famous 101 series and further confused matters by missing out a large block of numerals during the twenty-four-year production run which ended in 1986. The very latest guns have been numbered around 541000.

Remington were not much more helpful with their famous 1100 semi-auto. Guns imported from the mid-1960s until 1970 had German proof marks and an additional three- or four-digit number, different from the serial number, stamped on the left side of the receiver, towards the front. However, Hull Cartridge have records of the serial numbers of every gun sold through them over a long period, and so can provide the sale date to dealers.

The Russians apply some logic to the serial numbers of Baikals; the first two digits of most numbers signify the year of manufacture. Thus a gun with a number beginning 88 was made in 1988. However, some Baikal serial numbers begin with letters and there the rule does not apply.

Dating English-made guns is easy if the manufacturer is still in business, and top firms such as Purdey, Boss and Holland & Holland can always date a gun exactly from its serial number and often tell you much about its history. But if the maker is out of business it often depends on your luck: books specifically about English-made guns provide some lists of serial numbers and years and the sporting gun departments of the best London auction houses may be helpful too. Furthermore, there is now also quite a trade in the records of long-expired gunmakers, so a few telephone calls may track down the holders of the original paperwork, sometimes from much longer than a hundred years ago. Good hunting!

5 CHOKE AND WHAT IT MEANS

Early, muzzle-loading shotguns had barrels of totally parallel bore, and barrels of this type were also fitted to early break-action guns. As a consequence, the shotgun could also be used to fire a solid ball of lead, and it thus doubled as a gun which, in the far corners of the British Empire, could be used to shoot some surprisingly large and dangerous four-footed game.

However, the British gamebird shooter had little interest in how his gun would perform against a charging tiger, but he did want to extend his range slightly and concentrate the pattern of his shot. In parallel-bored guns it was common to do this by incorporating what was known as a concentrator in the cartridge. It was no more than a cylinder of card about half an inch long enclosing the forward end of the shot column, and concentrators for 12-bores were frequently made by utilizing half an inch cut from the front end of a 16-bore cartridge case. Remember that all cartridge cases were made of paper in those days. The concentrator travelled through the barrel with the shot charge and helped to hold it together as it issued into the atmosphere.

ENTER THE CHOKE

This tactic was a bit of a stop-gap until a new technology arrived, and credit for the invention of the choke-bored barrel is usually given to a Newcastle gunsmith named William Rochester Pape, who in 1866 patented the idea of a constriction built into the muzzle end of the barrel tube to funnel the shot into a denser pattern. The idea was further developed by the Birmingham gunmaker William Wellington Greener,

who had perfected the technique by 1875. Choke-bored barrels soon became popular and so a system of marking the degree of choke had to be developed.

The buyer of a gun obviously wanted to know how much choke was present in a barrel and thus the trade developed the descriptive system which still exists. A barrel with no choke at all is called 'true cylinder', or just 'cylinder'. An 'improved cylinder' barrel has 0.005in (0.127mm) of choke, and $^1/_4$ choke is a constriction of 0.010in (0.254mm). From there on, chokes go up in increments of 0.010in (0.245mm); thus half choke is 0.020in (0.508mm), $^3/_4$ is 0.030in (0.762mm), and full choke is 0.040in (1.016mm). Chokes may be made as tight as 0.050in (1.27mm) and these are usually known as 'extra full', although they are uncommon and have little practical use. I have seen them on some American trap guns and also on a few field models of eastern European manufacture, but in most cases these ultra-tight chokes offer little improvement in performance and may throw very poor patterns.

American guns, or guns intended for the American market, are usually marked differently. Their cylinder barrel is the same as ours, while their improved cylinder corresponds to our $^1/_4$. 'Modified' is the same as our $^1/_2$, and

The true definition of 'choke' is a comparison between the main barrel diameter and the bore at the muzzles. As barrel dimensions vary, even in guns with nominally the same bore, measurement with a bore micrometer is the only true way of checking the degree of choke.

improved modified is the same as our $^3/_4$. Full means the same on both sides of the Atlantic; while American sportsmen use extra full for turkey shooting and some trap applications. The American skeet choke usually has up to 0.005in (0.127mm) of constriction, although some are true cylinder, or anything in between.

European guns frequently use a system of star marks to signify the degree of choke. With this marking, ★ = full, ★★ = $^3/_4$, ★★★ = $^1/_2$, ★★★★ = $^1/_4$ and ★★★★★ = either cylinder or skeet. I have seen all sorts of variation on this star mark, from well-drawn six-pointed stars to things that look more like a letter 'Y' and even blobs. These markings often appear as small notches in the ends of multichoke tubes so that the degree of choke may be ascertained without taking the choke out of the gun.

MEASURING THE CHOKE

There is no easy way of measuring exactly how much choke is present in a barrel, for the simple reason that choke is a comparison between the diameter of the main bore of the gun and at the muzzles, and the exact internal diameter of barrels varies so much. The 'standard' internal diameter of a 12-bore barrel is 0.729in (18.517mm), but there are quite large differences from one gun to another. For instance, many old English shotguns were built with 12-

bore chambers and what were technically 13-bore barrels of 0.710in diameter or a little more, while many modern Italian shotguns, including most Berettas, have 0.719in barrels. At the other end of the scale are the over-bored barrels fitted to the Browning Ultras and some Miroku models. These are usually about 0.745in. In other words, the description '12-bore' can cover barrels varying in diameter within a range of 0.026in (0.66mm).

Much the same is true of other bores. The nominal diameter of a 16-bore is 0.662in, but they may vary all the way from 0.637 to 0.669in, and 20-bores, with a nominal diameter of 0.615in, range from 0.596 to 0.626in. With these smaller bores, diameters at the tighter end of the scale are rarely encountered, but there are a few around. So, if barrels are of varying diameters, then chokes must be too. The true measure of a choke is its comparison with the diameter of the main bore, so full choke in a 0.719in barrel will have a diameter of 0.679in, while in a 0.745in barrel it will be 0.705in. That is a variation of 0.026in, so, if you want to know what choke is in a gun it is clearly no good measuring the diameter across the end of the barrel.

What you have to do is to use a gunsmith's bore micrometer to measure both the bore and the choke and subtract the one from the other. Thus a gun that is 0.725in in the bore and 0.705in in the choke has 0.020in of choke or half choke. It sounds complicated but it is the

This is a gunsmith's bore micrometer, used to check the internal diameters of barrels and chokes.

only way to do it if you want to be exact. Fortunately, most bore micrometers work with a dial gauge; so that you just set the dial on zero in the main bore then read off the figure you get when the micrometer is in the choke.

Diameters stamped on barrels should not be trusted for exact precision. Modern, metric marks are accurate only within a tolerance of 0.2mm (0.008in), while markings in decimals of an inch were determined by relatively crude plug gauges and are even less accurate. Twelve-bore guns proofed in England before 1954 were marked 12/1 (0.740in), 12 (0.729in), 13/1 (0.719in) and 13 (0.710in). These markings, and similar-style markings on 16- and 20-bores are, again, too inaccurate for precision and may lead to inaccurate choke evaluation.

As if all this were not confusing enough, some barrels perform differently from others for no easily discernible reason, and the type of cartridge may make a big difference to the pattern diameter too. All of which leaves you with, fortunately, a very simple solution: you either scrounge the use of a pattern plate (many shooting grounds have them) or, more simply, pick up a load of cardboard boxes from the supermarket and open them out flat.

Patterning

If you are using the cardboard box method, take them to a field where you have permission to shoot and either lean them against a hedgerow or a couple of hay bales or pin them to a couple of poles driven into the ground. Whichever you prefer, make totally sure that the shooting background is safe because shot whistles through hedges and can even go through bales. Then measure out 30yd and shoot at your cardboard from there, using your favourite cartridge. The table below will help you to evaluate your patterns, and it comes courtesy of Eley Hawk.

I suggest 30yd because it is the minimum range at which you will easily tell the difference between 3/4 and full choke. Expect cartridges with felt or fibre wads to pattern slightly less tightly than those with cup-type plastic wads, and 24g competition cartridges designed for the international trap disciplines to pattern a little more tightly than you might expect.

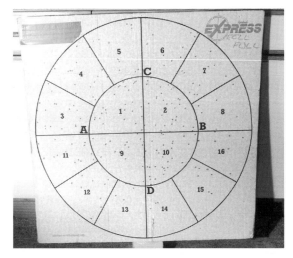

This full-choke pattern, shot at 30yd, contains virtually all of the shot in the cartridge.

Percentage of pellets in 30in circle				
Bore of cylinder	Range in yards			
	25	30	35	40
true cylinder	69	60	49	40
improved cylinder	82	72	60	50
1/4	87	77	65	55
1/2	94	83	71	60
3/4	100	91	77	65
full	100	100	84	70

If you have the use of a steel pattern plate, take with you a tin of white emulsion paint and a big brush. If you paint the plate between shots, the pellet strikes will show up as black or grey blobs. There is no need to wait for the paint to dry, although most brands of emulsion dry quickly out of doors on a warm day – so quickly that it is wise to take a can of water as well to keep the brush moist and to dilute the paint if it becomes too thick.

The best results come from taking the average of several shots through each choke. Do not draw your circle first and then fire at it, because you will never hit it in the middle. Rather, fire your pattern and then draw a 30in circle around the densest part. To save time in drawing circles, you could make up a 30in hoop of reasonably thick steel wire. If you tick off each pellet strike with a big red or black marker on paper, or on the steel plate by smearing over each strike with your finger end or a stick as you count it, you will not lose count so easily. When you have done this you will have the best possible evaluation of choke: you know the exact pattern your gun is shooting at an appropriate range, and you cannot have better information than that.

To begin with, the most accurate way of determining the number of pellets in a given cartridge is to take one to pieces and make a physical count. However, if you want to cheat, here are the numbers of common sizes of shot which make up 10g: size 5 = 78, size 6 = 95, size 7 = 120, size 7 $1/2$ = 140, size 8 = 160 and size 9 = 210. I have given the numbers per 10g rather than per ounce because it is easier on a calculator. For 24g loads you multiply by 2.4, for 30g by 3, and so on.

For a quick exercise, let us assume that you are patterning your gun at 30yd with 28g of No.6, which is 266 pellets. If 199 of them fall within your 30in circle, that is 74.8 per cent. Referring to the table above, we see that the true choke of the gun is somewhere between improved cylinder and $1/4$.

A really good pattern is one which is slightly denser towards the centre and with a minimal number of 'flyers', shot which fall well outside

the predicted area.

To form the best possible pattern – one which is even with no gaps through which targets can escape – shot has to emerge from the muzzle as truly round as possible, because pellets which have become distorted out of round have poor aerodynamic shape and do not fly true. We discuss this problem more fully in Chapter 11, but when evaluating a pattern, it is important to be able to visualize the shot cloud in the air.

The important thing to realize is that it is three-dimensional; not flat like a plate, but egg-shaped, the central cross-section of the 'egg' being dependent on the degree of choke. As the shot charge passes through the choke, some pellets come out travelling slightly faster than others, and the fastest, roundest pellets are those which lead the group. Over the years many efforts have been made to analyse the length and composition of patterns in the target area, and early attempts in the USA involved the firing of a stationary gun at a long target attached to the side of a moving vehicle. If the distances were accurately measured and the speed of both the shot and the vehicle were known, it was thereby possible to translate the flat image on the target into a three-dimensional picture. More recent, and much more accurate, evaluations have been made by Dr Roger Giblin, of University College, London, as part of his experiments to test the suitability of substitutes for lead. His test rig, on the Holland & Holland shooting ground in north London, checked the velocity of the shot at several points down-range and timed each individual pellet strike on the target by electronic means. Shot cloud evaluation has become an exact science.

SPECIAL CHOKES

Over the years special chokes have been produced for particular purposes. The once-popular retro-skeet choke, mentioned earlier, had a small, machined-out chamber behind the choke itself. Experiments have also been made with rifled chokes and chokes with internal

long chamber bored in muzzle has effect of
tightening choke

If the barrel walls are thick enough, a gunsmith can sometimes tighten a choke which is too loose by over-boring a long camber behind the muzzle.

retro-skeet
choke

The so-called 'retro-skeet' choke, not popular on modern guns, provides an open pattern for the close-target discipline.

ridges but, in practical terms, little has been done to improve the plain taper. Under British law as it stands, a rifled choke, however short, transforms a shotgun into a rifle and therefore makes it illegal for the owner to hold on a shotgun certificate.

The common gunsmithing task of relieving chokes is usually done with an adjustable reamer on a long shaft, introduced into the barrel from the breech end, final polishing taking place with a rotating hone. If internally chromium-plated barrels are to have their chokes widened, the chrome at the muzzle first has to be ground away – usually with a soft metal lap charged with a sharp abrasive powder.

A gunsmith can also sometimes achieve the apparently impossible and tighten the chokes on a fixed-choke gun. On barrels with sufficient wall thickness a long, over-bored chamber can be machined behind the muzzle. This effectively increases the bore of the gun and causes the existing choke to shoot tighter patterns.

The first commonly available multichoke system was introduced by Winchester in the late 1970s on their famous 101 series of guns. They

called it the 'Winchoke' and it was an available option on most models from 1981 onwards. Browning, Miroku and Beretta, as well as a host of other gunmakers, soon followed the Winchester example, and even Holland & Holland now produce a sporter with multichokes by the American specialists Briley.

Most early multichoke tubes had an external, knurled collar which protruded from the end of the muzzle. This made them easy to screw in and out, but they spoiled the lines of a gun and so later tubes were made with castellated notches cut into the ends of the tubes so that they could be inserted and withdrawn with a key. This system looks far better in that the ends of the tubes are hidden, but it may lead to over-tightening if an over-large key is supplied.

A fixed-choke gun can usually be converted to a multichoke by specialists in the United Kingdom such as Nigel Teague and Pro Choke. All that is required is that the gun has sufficient barrel wall thickness at the muzzles to accept the threaded inserts. The tubes are made only after the internal barrel measurement has been checked, so that the chokes are tailor-made for each individual gun and thus are always true to their marking. They are usually manufactured from non-rusting stainless steel and can be made to be fitted with a tapered key so that they are completely invisible when inserted. Such chokes can be made to shoot in any feasible pattern the customer requires, and they generally shoot better patterns than factory-fitted chokes.

American specialists such as Briley, Rhino and Kicks Industries make alternative tubes which may be fitted to guns which have been manufactured as multichokes, and many of these available types protrude from the ends of the barrels and include ported sections. The purpose of these ports is to provide jets of hot gas which are deflected upwards, sideways or backwards at the moment of firing, the idea being that they stabilize the gun, cut recoil and damp down muzzle flip. Their main popularity is for skeet shooting, in which a well-controlled first shot from a stable gun means that the second target in the doubles can be acquired very

Multichoke tubes should be kept clean, with lightly greased threads, and discarded if they are ever knocked out of round.

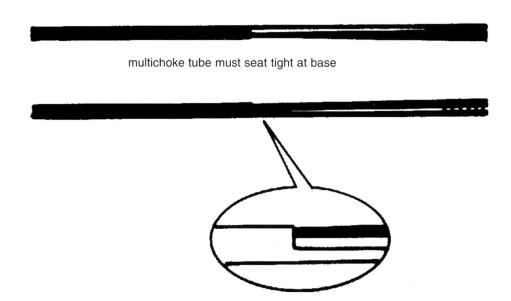

multichoke tube must seat tight at base

A multichoke tube must seat tight at its base and provide a gas seal to prevent debris from being blown into the threads. The presence of grease on the outside of the tube helps in this regard.

quickly. And, of course, an improved pattern ensures cleaner breaks.

Specialist companies will also cut ports in the barrels themselves, the idea again being to stabilize the gun at the moment of firing. When this modification is done, a series of usually upward-facing holes is machined in the forward ends of the barrels, usually by spark erosion so that there is no internal burring. Guns provided with factory porting include the now-discontinued Winchester 8500 Trap, certain Miroku skeet models and some Beretta sporters.

It should be noted that guns which have been modified from fixed-choke to multichoke and those which have had porting work done on the barrels should always be resubmitted for proof before they are resold.

6 RECOIL AND HOW TO TAME IT

WHAT IT IS AND HOW IT ARISES

Recoil and its causes and effects are the subjects of constant debate among shooters. Everyone seems to be seeking the ultimate – a high-performance cartridge which offers so little recoil that you hardly feel it go off, and it is an impossible dream. It is also true that more shooters than you would ever believe suffer from recoil problems, and it is nothing to do with the physical size or strength of the sufferer. The human frame was not meant to be bashed painfully in the shoulder in the name of enjoyment – which is what shooting should be.

One of Newton's laws of motion dictates that if you apply force to a body (such as firing a projectile) then there is going to be an equal and opposite reaction to that force (recoil). All the gun and cartridge designers between them can do is to damp that force as well as they are able and apply the recoil force to the shooter's shoulder in such a way that he or she suffers the minimum of discomfort. That is the theory, anyway, but what about the practice?

Another of Newton's laws states that motion, once begun, will continue indefinitely in a frictionless world until acted upon by another force, as a result of which the energy in the moving body will be converted into some other form. A motor car weighing a ton and travelling at 60mph would continue to travel at that speed for ever on a level surface if it were not for friction with the air, the rolling resistance of the tyres and internal friction and drag within the machinery. Even with those factors, if allowed to free-wheel, the car travels for a considerable distance before it comes to rest. If we wish to slow it down more quickly than that we have to apply a mechanical device to disperse the kinetic energy. A braking system applies controlled friction which turns the energy of motion into heat and gets rid of it by radiating it away into the atmosphere. The atmosphere thereby becomes a little warmer but the energy is still present. It has not been destroyed, just converted into another form. Brakes are a simple means of getting rid of unwanted motion. What a pity there is nothing so simple which can be applied to the recoiling movement of a gun; instead we have to look further – both into physics and the nature of the human nervous system.

WHAT CAN BE DONE

An ounce of shot at a muzzle velocity of 1,400 ft/sec possesses over 1,900ft/lb of energy and forces equal to those which imparted that energy to the shot are transmitted backwards into the gun. How can we cope with this? First of all we can make the gun heavy, because a heavy gun will not be moved so far nor so fast as a light one for a given amount of energy. Compare that with the car again: the engine in a normal production car weighing about a ton, applied at full power for a minute, will propel it forward at a maximum speed of about 100mph. If we put that same engine in a car twice as heavy and drive flat out for a minute both the maximum speed and the acceleration would be cut drastically.

Put simply, gun weight soaks up recoil, so it is something we can use within practical limits. Those limits are usually dictated by the style of shooting for which the gun is designed: a gun for the trap disciplines may weigh 8lb or a little

RECOIL AND HOW TO TAME IT

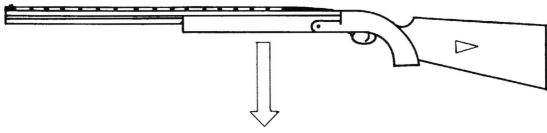

A heavy gun soaks up recoil better than a light one.

more, while a gun which has to be carried all day in the field is going to be unduly cumbersome if it weighs much more than 7lb.

Fitting the Gun to the Shooter

The next thing we can do is to make the gun fit the shooter. This will not reduce the recoil in any way, but it will distribute the recoil forces properly so that they can be best absorbed by the physical frame. A gun which fits properly only feels as if it recoils less because the recoil is applied to the shoulder through the muscle groups best suited to absorb it. Gun fit, then, not only helps us to shoot straighter but more comfortably too.

Another thing we can do is to fit the gun with a thick recoil pad made of a material of a consistency which will absorb the rearward movement of the gun as it compresses. It is like inserting a small, damped spring between the gun and the shooter, but it has its drawbacks too. Such pads are invariably made of either rubber or a rubber-like plastic which means that, if they are soft enough to do the job, they are also soft enough to be 'clingy' against clothing. This means that guns so fitted can be slow and awkward to mount to the shoulder quickly; so thick, springy pads are usually fitted only to guns intended for the trap disciplines, in which the target is called for with the gun ready-mounted to the shoulder.

This idea of a 'spring' between the gun and the shooter was taken one step further by an American development a few years ago. A company developed a two-part stock sprung by a

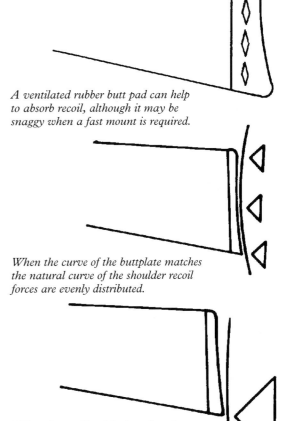

A ventilated rubber butt pad can help to absorb recoil, although it may be snaggy when a fast mount is required.

When the curve of the buttplate matches the natural curve of the shoulder recoil forces are evenly distributed.

When the profile of the buttplate does not match the curve of the shoulder or when a gun with a prominent toe is accidentally mounted too high, all the recoil may be concentrated at one localized point, with consequential pain.

damped gas strut which actually came from an estate car tailgate. When the gun fired the whole stock compressed, but, for comfort, the cheek-piece remained stationary. It certainly damped recoil, but the rearward movement of the gun by – as I remember it – up to an inch on firing, was certainly a peculiar sensation. The idea never caught on.

Clothing Padding

On the practical side, one cheap solution is to add a little padding to your clothing. You will notice that, when shooting in the winter, the presence of a thick pullover under your jacket eases recoil quite considerably. You will not want to have to wear thick clothing in a heat-wave, but you can apply localized padding. My skeet vest was made with a small pocket on the inside, in the area of the right shoulder and an ordinary handkerchief, folded so as to just fit the pocket, reduces perceived recoil quite considerably. When I am testing cartridges for *Sporting Gun* magazine I often have to fire long strings of shots with powerful cartridges, so on testing sessions I always make sure that I have that particular skeet vest with me. It saves me from endless bruises.

Using Human Physiology

The next thing we can do is to take advantage of a quirk of the human nervous system which prevents us from appreciating quite what is going on if events happen extremely quickly. For example, the least painful way to remove a patch of sticking plaster from your skin is to snatch it off as fast as you possibly can. The body does not seem to register pain which may be quite intense so long as its duration is short enough. Most people would apply the same principle if they got a wood splinter in a finger: yank it out quickly and it doesn't hurt, pull it out slowly and it does.

This principle may also be applied to the way in which we feel the forces of recoil. Make the recoil sharp and fast enough and it is not felt in the same way as it would be if it were more prolonged. We are talking about differences of only

milliseconds here, but the principle seems to work. It is achieved by using propellant powders with an accelerated burn rate.

The late Gough Thomas had something to say about it in his book *Shotguns and Cartridges for Game and Clays* (A.& C. Black, London; last revised by the author in 1987). He recalled experiments performed by Eley in which batches of cartridges were prepared with identical shot weights and velocities; the only difference being that, by using different powder/primer combinations, some batches accelerated the shot to its muzzle velocity more quickly than others. The recoil forces involved therefore had to be the same; but those with the faster powders would deliver them in the form of a short, sharp burst of energy while the slower powders would deliver them as a longer 'shove' rather than a quick blow. A group of shooters all identified the faster-burning cartridges, although all the cases and heads were similarly marked, and said that they were much more comfortable to shoot. The only assumption which may be made is that the short, sharp shock is less painful than the slower shove, even though the energy imparted is the same.

This is borne out by personal experience. A few years ago I was keen to do some experiments with $7/_8$oz game cartridges and so I asked a company to load some for me. I asked for what I thought was the impossible – long-range cartridges with very light recoil. In terms of recoil they were among the most comfortable I have ever fired, yet the pressures were quite high and the muzzle velocities were well in excess of 1,400 ft/sec. The powder was very fine, like dust, with an exceptionally fast burn rate. This was further proof that a fast burn equals a low perceived recoil.

Unfortunately, it is possible to pursue the 'fast burn' approach only so far. You can use it with light loads but, as the weight of shot increases, you have to go for slower-burning powders. Heavy shotloads have more inertia and therefore need to be accelerated to ballistic speeds more gradually if the pressure in the breech of the gun is not to go beyond acceptable limits.

For this reason heavy cartridges are always going to produce a high perceived recoil.

Learning from Painful Experience

There are also other factors to be taken into account, both physical and psychological. Put simply, if you have been told that something you have never experienced before is going to hurt you, you will be conditioned to expect pain. Asked for a snap reaction after firing their first-ever shot with a 12-bore, most people will say that they found it painful because popular belief has it that a 12-bore hurts your shoulder; yet, fortunately, most are keen to try again. After a few shots the recoil does not seem to bother them so much and they often forget it in the excitement of seeing their first target break against the sky. Excitement also dulls our perception of pain. Sportsmen and women, when hot and excited, may suffer some quite severe injuries and not feel pain at the time – it is one of nature's devices to help us to fight our way out of tight corners. A shooter in an exciting situation may acquire quite severe shoulder bruises which are noticed only when in the shower at the end of the day.

As experience grows, people also get used to the way in which they must position their bodies and tense their muscles in order to receive recoil in the most comfortable way. Newcomers are always told to lean into the gun with most of their weight on the forward foot, and to tuck the stock tightly into the shoulder. Some do and some do not, but those who do as they are told find the first few shots a much less painful experience. There are also finer points which a newcomer teaches himself or herself as experience is gained. This learning experience is not unique to the shooting sports. For instance, martial arts enthusiasts soon learn how to fall in the most comfortable way and parachutists learn how to absorb the shocks of landing without hurting themselves. Contrast these experiences to your feelings when you first fell off your bicycle as a child and you will see what I mean: an unexpected fall, when you land awkwardly, is always painful. A controlled fall, when you know what

is happening and know how to prepare your body, hurts less or not at all. You can teach your body to absorb shock without undue discomfort – you learn to 'ride the punches'.

To sum up so far: if you find recoil uncomfortable you can take the following measures:

• Shoot a light or relatively low-performance cartridge through a heavy gun.
• Get a good instructor or gun fitter to check that you are mounting your gun properly and that it fits you.
• Fit a soft recoil pad, provided that it is not going to impede your style.
• Insert a little padding into the shoulder of your shooting jacket. It must be carefully positioned and not be so thick as to impede gun mount or make your jacket feel 'lumpy' and awkward.
• Experiment with different cartridges with the same published performance, because some give lower perceived recoil than others, usually due to the burn rate of the powder.
• Do not despair if you have just had your first lesson and found it painful – there is still a lot of learning to do, and things will get easier.

MODIFYING THE GUN

There are other aspects of gun construction which are claimed to relieve recoil slightly. One is to make the barrel slightly greater in its diameter than its nominal bore: say 0.745in rather than 0.729. This is the recipe used in the Browning Ultra series of guns and also in some Miroku models. The increase in comfort is slight but it is there: if you just put the gun to your shoulder and fire it you will hardly notice the difference, but you may well be less fatigued after a long string of shots. Machining a more gradual taper into the forcing cones – the areas where the chambers taper into the barrels – has a slight, similar effect.

There are also a number of 'recoil reducing' devices on the market, most of them from the USA, which take the form of metal cylinders which can be placed in the stock bolt hole of an O/U or in the magazine tube of a semi-automatic. Most are sealed units and one is not supposed to know what goes on inside them, but most contain a sliding weight controlled by a damped spring. It is also true that most have a pretty minimal effect, although the extra weight may be useful provided that it does not throw the gun off balance. It is significant that one importer told me that he had stopped bringing in a particular model from the USA 'because it didn't work'.

CHANGE YOUR GUN?

Another real answer to taming recoil is to shoot a semi-automatic shotgun rather than a break-action. Gas-fed semi-automatics are the best in this respect, and their automatic reloading from the magazine tube works by tapping high-pressure gas from the midpoint of the barrel at the moment of firing and using it to cycle a piston working inside a cylinder. This gas relief lessens the recoil a little, and I would guess that the reciprocating motion of the piston, the relatively heavy bolt and the linking mechanism between them help too.

Whatever you do, do not fall for the chestnut that 'a 20-bore recoils less than a 12-bore.' It does not: reducing the size of the barrel bore makes no difference at all to the recoil, and 20-bores recoil less than 12s only if they are relatively heavy (7lb or more) and are used with the light, $^{13}/_{16}$oz load. A full ounce of shot through a 20-bore recoils just as much as it does through a 12-bore, and through the usually lighter 20-bore gun it is going to hurt more. In most cases you would be better off shooting a light load (say 24g or $^7/_8$oz) through a 12-bore, and the ammunition would be cheaper too.

All of the above assumes that the recoil pain is felt in the shoulder. A minority of shooters complain that they are being hit in the face by the stock and have tender bruises along the jawbone or on the cheekbone to prove it. These maybe caused by a gun which, for a variety of reasons, develops more than the usual muzzle flip – maybe as the result of a powerful cartridge being fired through a very light-barrelled gun. A more usual cause is poor gun fit, and the fitter's frequent solution is to shave down the stock so that it has a forward slope, away from the cheek. Thus the shooter can hold the stock to the cheek while the shot is fired, but on the recoil it will move away slightly.

A FINAL WORD

Finally, if you do suffer from recoil pain do something about it! There is nothing to be ashamed of and it is certainly nothing to do with physical size or build. Some strapping six-footers suffer and some shorter, slimmer people do not. There is also nothing heroic or even advantageous in shooting the most powerful cartridges you can buy: use the load best suited to the job in hand. If you still suffer some of these recommended measures should be helpful, and remember above all that shooting is supposed to be pleasure not pain.

7 REPEATING SHOTGUNS

EARLY MODELS

The concept of a repeating shotgun is not new. The Americans had a pump-action repeater – the Spencer – more than a hundred years ago and it was introduced to Britain by the gunmaking firm of Charles Lancaster & Co. in 1882. Lancaster fitted the guns with English-style Damascus barrels in the hope that they would be more readily accepted and set about the business of convincing the conservative, game-shooting gentry that they could use the extra firepower. They were not very interested, and the pump-action even then had the lack of popularity that it still retains in the United Kingdom. This is probably to do with the numbers of them in military, special forces and police use throughout the world and their 'Rambo' image.

The pump action was all well and good in technical terms and it is still the most reliable of the repeating actions; but you have to work the mechanism by hand and what inventors were really seeking was a gun which would reload itself from a magazine every time the shooter pulled the trigger until the magazine was empty. This is known as a semi-automatic action, a full automatic action being one which fires repetitively all the time the trigger is kept pulled back, like a machine-gun. The first practicable semi-automatic shotgun was the long-recoil Browning Auto 5, designed by John Moses Browning at the end of the last century. Sensing that he was on a winner, the Mormon from Utah took the gun to Winchester for its production for the American market, but had an argument with the company over royalties. He arranged for world-market production to be put in the hands of Fabrique Nationale in Belgium – the firm which

was eventually to become FN Browning and produce some of the world's most desirable O/U shotguns. American production went to Remington, who called the gun the 11A.

Browning are still building the Auto 5 in Belgium, while Remington dropped their version in 1948. Over the long years of its production the patent was officially shared by Breda, Beretta, Franchi and Savage, among others, and pirated by more than a few makers world-wide as well. There is even a legally-built, Japanese Auto 5 look-alike. It was the ultimate shotgun of its type and still has its loyal band of enthusiasts. There are not many to be seen in the United Kingdom, but there are even custom-built versions with gold encrustation.

Action

The Auto 5 and its look-alikes have successive cartridges cycled into the chamber by the recoil of the preceding shot. When the first shot is fired the barrel assembly, which runs on bushes and is held forward by a coil spring running concentrically with the magazine tube, recoils and compresses the spring. At the same time the bolt is unlocked and its inertia frees it from the barrel, ejecting the spent cartridge case. Once springs have tamed the recoil forces, the components start to move back into their original positions. As the bolt moves forward it picks up the second cartridge, which the preceding motion has freed from the magazine tube and transferred to a carrier. Once the bolt slams shut and locks, the hammer and trigger have been reset and the gun is ready to fire again.

This action requires a recoil of well over an inch to make it work properly, and to produce this recoil it needs a relatively powerful cartridge. The Auto 5 is generally not happy with a shell carrying less than 32g (1¹/₈oz) of shot and most will not work reliably with a lighter load. It also has a rather odd action when fired, until one gets used to it, and the fact that the barrel moves backwards when you pull the trigger can be quite disconcerting. An alternative, short-recoil system, in which the chamber recoils about a tenth of an inch, is slightly more tolerant of lighter loads but has never really made the grade in world popularity.

Most modern semi-autos are gas-fed, cycled by high-pressure gas tapped from the barrel at the moment of firing. They work like this: as the wad passes the midpoint of the barrel it passes over a small gas port or ports (usually two); these vent part of the following column of high-pressure gas into an annular piston which surrounds the magazine tube. Inside this cylinder is a piston which is attached to the bolt by a linkage which runs parallel to the magazine tube. The first part of the piston's movement unlocks a latch securing the bolt to a rearward extension of the barrel, and the rest of the movement gives the bolt a smart push backwards. The gas in the cylinder, having done its work, is vented to the atmosphere through slots or holes in the fore-end.

The bolt, as it continues to move backwards under its own inertia, extracts the spent cartridge case with a claw and flicks it out through the loading port. When it reaches the back limit of its travel a fresh cartridge, which has been transferred from the magazine on to a carrier, is placed in front of the bolt. The bolt then moves forward under the pressure of a spring it has compressed on its backward journey, pushing the cartridge before it into the chamber. The final movement re-engages the latch between the bolt and the barrel extension. During these movements the trigger mechanism has been recocked, ready to fire the next shot.

CURRENT MODELS

Guns working on this principle are currently

available, for instance, from Beretta, Browning, Remington, Fabarm, Lanber, Mossberg and Winchester. The degree of sophistication they embody depends largely on the price you pay, and many of the more expensive guns have a mechanism which allows them to cycle on a wide range of ammunition. It generally consists of a spring-loaded gas valve built into the operating piston, so that any possible over-pressure created by a powerful cartridge is vented into the atmosphere before it can force the piston back at a greater speed than that for which the mechanism was designed and thus cause premature wear to the gun and discomfort to the shooter. On cheaper guns the mechanism is usually tuned to a range of cartridges, those with magnum chambers working best with powerful goose shells. However, guns which require a powerful cartridge can usually be regulated to accept something lighter – generally by slightly boring out the gas ports. Few 12-bore guns will cycle reliably on shot loads lighter than 28g (1oz) unless they have been specifically regulated to do so, and none that I have ever tested will work with low-powered, subsonic ammunition. For training purposes, however, they may be fed with one cartridge at a time.

ANOTHER MODE OF OPERATION

There is a third method of operating a semi-auto, usually known as 'inertia', although it is entirely recoil-dependent. It is commonly found on Benelli guns and works like this: the bolt is in two parts, a relatively light, turning head and a relatively heavy body. Lugs on the turning head engage with grooves in the mouth of the chamber, like those on a bolt-action rifle. When the gun recoils the main body of the bolt tends to stay still, compressing a spring between the body and the head and, at the same time, turning the bolt head so that it disengages from the chamber mouth. The spring then takes over and forces the bolt and its head back to eject the empty case and cycle the second shell from the magazine tube. It is ingenious, and works very

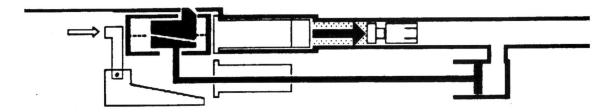

Firing cycle of a gas-fed, semi-automatic shotgun. The bolt is in its fully-forward position and is locked to the barrel extension. The trigger has been pulled, the hammer has fallen and the shot and wad are on their way up the barrel.

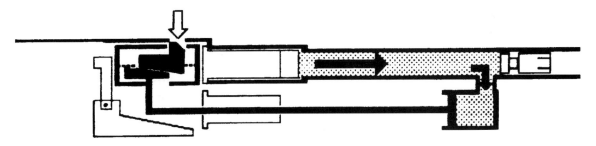

The wad has now passed the gas port, and high-pressure gas has started to move the piston back. A rod attached to the piston has unlocked the bolt, leaving it free to travel backwards.

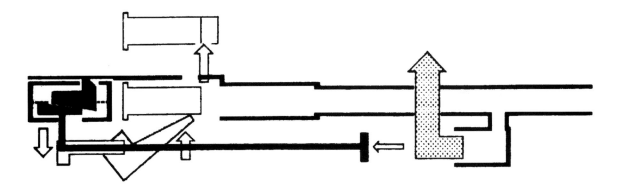

The piston has now come out of the cylinder, allowing gas to be vented into the atmosphere. The shot has gone and the bolt is fully back. An extractor claw on the bolt has pulled out the spent cartridge, and an ejector has flipped it out through the loading port. The hammer has been recocked and a fresh cartridge lifted from the magazine tube. When a spring drives the bolt forward, the cartridge will be chambered and the gun will be ready to fire again.

smoothly with a wide variety of cartridge loadings.

The mechanism is also compact and, as there is no gas piston or spring surrounding the magazine tube, the fore-end can be very slim. There are also a minimum number of parts whizzing about in the milliseconds after a shot is fired, and this makes the loading smooth and reliable. As a by-product, there are fewer components to clean than on many semi-automatics and no problems through hard carbon building up around gas ports and piston assembles. During reloading the spent case is gripped by extractor claws in the bolt head and drawn backwards until the rim engages with a small, spring-loaded plunger in the barrel extension. The plunger flips the 'empty' out through the ejection port.

AMMUNITION PREFERENCES

Many semi-automatics are notoriously fussy about their diet and will sometimes cycle perfectly on one particular cartridge yet fail to do so with another brand which generates the same power. The speed at which the cartridge reaches its pressure peak may be part of the problem, as is the actual pressure present in the barrel as the wad passes the gas ports; but a big factor is the profile of the rim on the cartridge head. If the rim is shallow or rounded it may slip from beneath the extractor claw before it has been fully withdrawn from the chamber and in this position will not allow the next cartridge to be cycled. A frequent symptom of this is that the gun sticks with the bolt fully back with the spent cartridge case laying loose in front of it. The solution, if you have a 'sticky' automatic, is first to change your ammunition. To what? Different guns seem to like different cartridges, but I have never known an automatic hang up on Winchester ammunition, and most shells loaded in Fiocchi cases are quite good too. This is not favouritism and there are other brands which are equally reliable, but you will have to experiment to find what suits your particular gun.

SHOOTING PROTOCOL, SAFETY AND OTHER MATTERS

As we discussed in the previous chapter, the semi-automatic offers the shooter a lower perceived recoil than a break-action gun and is therefore often more suitable for women and lightly built men. The semi-automatic is perfectly acceptable on the clay ground and for pigeon, wildfowl and all casual shooting. However, it is generally not acceptable on formal or even walked-up game shoots, and so if this is your preference you are advised to stick to a break-action. If, for reasons of the recoil, you have to shoot one and wish to go to a formal game shoot then explain the reasons either to your potential host or the shoot manager beforehand. In the circumstances you may be given permission to bring your automatic, particularly if you are suffering from some disability, but do not be surprised if you are not. Game shooting is still a very conservative sport, with strictly held traditions.

Many shooters distrust semi-autos on safety grounds, and it is true that on a casual glance you cannot tell whether a semi-auto is loaded or not, unlike a break-action gun which, when broken, can be seen to be unloaded and safe. This problem usually manifests itself when you are carrying a semi-auto on a shooting ground, but there is an answer to it. It is possible to buy a chamber-blocking device which consists of a cartridge-shaped plug with a very long head which holds the bolt back. To advertise its presence the plug usually has a strip of coloured ribbon attached to its head; this hangs out of the loading port for all to see. With such a plug fitted, not only is the gun known to be safe and without a cartridge in the chamber, but, while the plug is present, it is impossible for a cartridge in the magazine tube to be transferred into the chamber. The plug is so constructed that it cannot be ejected by the gun's ejection mechanism, and the only way in which the gun will begin to work again is when the bolt is pulled fully back and the plug removed by hand. This is done only on the firing point, when the shooter is facing in a safe direction and ready to load and call for a target. Another way of signifying that a semi-automatic is empty and safe is to take a yellow duster and force as much as possible of it into the chamber and the area in front of the bolt. This leaves a long, yellow tail sticking out of the loading port and, again, stops a cartridge being cycled from the magazine tube and provides an easily seen indication that the gun is safe. Autos, of course, should not be carried with cartridges in the magazine tube, and anything that blocks the chamber and the mechanism is a second line of defence, like a safety catch.

The semi-auto has a further disadvantage over a break-action in that a conventional, right-handed gun is not totally adaptable for use by left-handers. Stocks can be bent to a left-handed profile or angled over by shims; but the loading port remains on the right and spits out fired cases across the shooter's face. This is usually distracting and annoying rather than dangerous, although I did meet one left-handed shooter who nearly set a luxuriant beard on fire with a spent cartridge case which came out with a slight flash of flame at its mouth! The only real solution for a left-hander is to buy a true left-handed gun which has been built as a mirror-image of a right-hander. Because of the obvious tooling costs involved for a minority market,

some manufacturers do not make a true left-hander, and, when they are available, they are usually more expensive.

As has been mentioned before, if a semi-auto is to be held on a British shotgun certificate it must have a fixed magazine tube which is capable of holding no more than two cartridges. In competition terms the ability to fire this third shot makes no difference, except in some 'flush' competitions where semi-auto users are often required to shoot in a class of their own, but it may be useful in a pigeon or duck hide, or when performing gamekeeping duties. But do not think that a three-shot auto, or even a five-shot one held on a firearms certificate, is going to increase your rate of fire dramatically over more than a few shots. Generally speaking, a break-action gun is faster to load and fire repetitively and, unless you are very well practised, there may be a huge 'fumble factor' in reloading an auto quickly. The secret, if there is one, is to buy an auto only if you really need one. Sensitivity to recoil is by far the most common justification. Cheapness used to be, but the trend is for a good semi-auto to cost nearly as much as a break-action of similar build quality. In safety terms, the semi-auto is neither more nor less dangerous than a gun with any other action. The important thing with an auto is to be seen to be safe.

8 WHEN THINGS GO WRONG

If you take a shooting safety officer's course you are taught to deal with gun malfunctions quickly and efficiently. This is an important skill: the situation in which a gun goes 'click' instead of 'bang' is potentially dangerous because an inexperienced shooter may completely lose his concentration and turn around to face you with a loaded gun. A loaded gun which has failed to fire may be particularly dangerous for all sorts of reasons, and that is why a good referee, instructor or safety officer keeps a particularly wary eye – and ear – open for gun malfunctions. When shooting alone or in the field you are your own safety officer, and you have to take the appropriate action without help.

A CAUTIONARY TALE

When you are teaching a newcomer to shoot, the best and safest place to be is relatively close behind his or her shooting shoulder – usually the right one. The position gives you a good view of how your pupil is performing and also enables you to take complete control of the situation if something goes wrong. You need do nothing more than lean forward to physically prevent the person from turning round and you can, if necessary, quickly put a controlling hand on the gun. That is why instructors stand close, and so do good referees if they suspect that the shooter is inexperienced.

I had never had to take a gun from anyone until one day when I had volunteered for some informal refereeing at a club skeet practice shoot. One of my squad was shooting a semi-auto and all went well until we got round to peg 6. When he called for the high bird his gun refused to fire and he just continued his left-to-right swing and, at the same time, started to move his feet. Convinced that he was going to turn around with a loaded gun, I stepped forward smartly and blocked his movement, at the same time reaching round with my right hand and grabbing the gun by the fore-end. He swore at me, then, realizing what he had done – or possibly looked like doing, he apologized and handed me the gun in a safe manner.

I could immediately see that the bolt of the gun, although it looked closed, was not quite – by about an eighth of an inch. I tried to pull it back and it was jammed solid. So there we were, with a loaded gun in an unknown, dangerous condition. In such cases you need to give yourself thinking time, so I asked the squad to stand back while I kept the gun pointed safely down-range and applied the safety catch. In such circumstances one expert is enough, there is no need for a committee, and things may get doubly confused in a crowd.

After a few moments of thought I gave the bolt handle a firm tug and it moved back about half an inch before jamming solid again; but this was enough for me to see that the ejector claw had snapped off and that the primer in the cartridge had not been struck by the firing pin. From there on it was relatively easy, while still keeping the gun pointed down-range, to undo the magazine tube cap and withdraw both the barrel and the live cartridge. At that point the gun was totally safe, and all of my advisers could contribute their pennyworths.

What I subsequently discovered was that, on the previous shot, the extractor claw had shattered and a sharp steel splinter from it had, by some quirk, lodged in the track along which the bolt travels. It had jammed the bolt on the next time it had come forward, just short of its lock-up point; thus, when the hammer fell, the firing pin did not reach the cartridge. The gun was in a safer condition than I had thought, but you never know these things at the time.

I tell this story to emphasize the importance of giving yourself a moment for reflection when you are faced with a gun or cartridge malfunction, or even if a shot feels strange for any reason. Keep the gun pointed down-range and safe while you think out the next move, then break it and look through the barrels before you reload.

ANOTHER STORY

I have another story about a man who did not do this and suffered the consequences. I had just written a piece in *Sporting Gun* about the dangers of a shot which produces little or no recoil and a very subdued report. It could be caused by a cartridge with either no propellant powder, or only a little, and insufficient energy to expel the wad from the barrel. If you load and fire another shot with a blocked barrel, the barrel will almost certainly burst. That month's magazine had been published when I received a telephone call from a chap who had an amazing tale of coincidence to tell.

He had gone to a clay shoot with a brand-new Lanber he had just bought and had not had time to read his magazine, which had been delivered that morning. All had gone well until he'd fired a shot which he described as 'virtually silent – kind of funny'. Without looking down the barrel he had reloaded and fired again, and the lower barrel of the gun had exploded just in front of his forward hand. Both barrels and the fore-end were completely wrecked, and neither he nor I could work out how he, and a number of bystanders too, had not been badly injured. He got away with a severe fright and what he described as a severe stinging sensation in his left hand which persisted for several hours. When he got home he read his *Sporting Gun* and realized what had happened: a lesson

learned the hard way.

If a shot generates far more recoil than you would expect from a particular cartridge, then the gun should be checked very carefully before it is loaded and fired again. Be particularly careful to check the barrel for bulges and check the jointing for looseness. Of course, it could be that both barrels of the gun fired together, which is a fault which must be referred to a gunsmith. I have to say that over-charged or double-charged cartridges are extremely rare and just do not get through the automatic checking on modern loading machinery. I would guess that most problems of this type occur through careless hand loading – either with too much powder or with a grade of powder unsuitable for the shot load.

MALFUNCTIONS

Now let us look at a few potential gun malfunctions, some of which may be dangerous. The others are just annoying, but possibly expensive to put right.

Misfires
If you get a click instead of a bang when you pull the trigger the first suspect is a cartridge with a dud or over-hard primer. However, there is a rare condition called a 'hang-fire' in which a faulty primer fires a few seconds after it has been struck. Therefore, after a click, it is customary safety practice to wait with the gun pointed in a safe direction for 30sec. If the cartridge has not fired in that time it may be deemed safe and may then be ejected.

This condition is extremely unusual but it does happen. I can recall that there was once an incident on a skeet range when a misfire was ejected prematurely and it went off just as the ejector was lifting it from the barrel. The shooter and the rest of the squad were not badly hurt, but they were showered with hot bits of cartridge and very badly frightened. So, if you get a misfire, wait before you reload. The most dangerous time for a cartridge to fire is just as you are opening the gun, while it is still fully in the barrel.

The appearance of a misfired cartridge is able to tell you a lot about what caused the problem. If the primer has been struck cleanly in the centre and the indentation is of the depth you would expect on a fired case, then the primer simply has not gone off. If the primer is lightly indented and the head of the cartridge is slightly dished inwards, then you have a hard primer. This, like all cartridge malfunctions, is comparatively rare, but the whole batch may be hard so other cartridges in the same box may give the same problem. If this is so, then tell the manufacturer because he will wish to take up the business of hard primers with his supplier.

A firing pin should make a clean, sharp indent in a primer. This one is slightly off-centre, but still good.

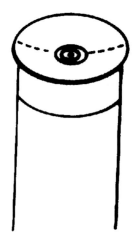

A cartridge with an over-hard primer is usually ejected with evidence of an apparently very light firing pin strike and a dished-in head.

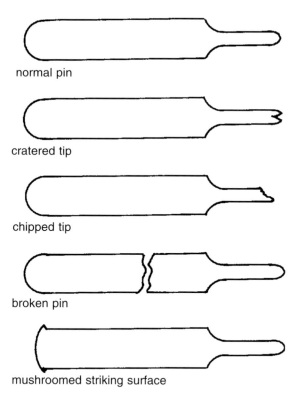

normal pin

cratered tip

chipped tip

broken pin

mushroomed striking surface

Firing pin faults: a firing pin should have a smoothly rounded tip. Cratered tips usually continue to fire, but may break at any time. These, and chipped tips, can usually be detected by looking down the firing pin holes. A pin broken along its length may cause intermittent firing faults. A pin which has become mushroomed at the back delivers lighter and lighter strikes until the gun refuses to fire.

Firing Pins

If the primer is lightly indented and the head is not dished, then the chances are that it has been struck only very lightly by the firing pin. Possibly the main spring driving the tumbler on that barrel is getting 'tired' and needs to be replaced or it could even be broken. The coil springs fitted to most modern guns will often continue to deliver strikes of low power even when they are broken in several pieces. Another cause may be a firing pin which has started to burr over at its back end. Even a firing pin broken into two can sometimes deliver a light strike, and a rarer cause is a lot of dirt in the mechanism. I once cured a mysterious, intermittent misfire by removing a tiny piece of lint from a cleaning rag which had dropped back down the firing pin hole in the breech face of one of my guns; this was stopping the firing pin from moving fully forward.

If the shallow strike is of an irregular shape then there may be a chip broken off the tip of the firing pin. If the strike is very broad and flat then the firing pin tip may have burred over or cracked off. I have also known a fragmented firing-pin return spring to cause light strikes by jamming the pin in its hole.

Springs and pins may almost be regarded as consumable parts of guns. Certainly they should last for many thousands of cartridges, but breakages, unless they are frequent, are no real reflection on gun quality. Most springs and pins can be replaced cheaply and quickly.

Triggers

All this assumes that you have actually heard or felt the click of the hammer, or tumbler, falling. If you have not then the trigger mechanism could be broken or the gun could be failing to cock. The most likely suspects here are broken or burred-over sears, cocking rods which are broken, bent or jammed, or a safety catch which is just failing to move into the fully-off position.

A quite common problem with many over-and-unders is that they will fire the first barrel quite satisfactorily, but the trigger will not transfer to the second. This is because, on most guns, the recoil of the first shot transfers the trigger action by moving an inertia block within the mechanism and – for some reason – the block has failed to move far enough.

There may be many causes: the first is dirt and old, sticky oil in the mechanism. Then there is the possibility of burred or bent components, or perhaps the cartridge is simply not powerful enough. This last fault was experienced by quite a lot of shooters when the standard clay load was dropped from 32g to 28, and the answer was for a gunsmith either to regulate the inertia block spring or replace it with a lighter one.

The shooter may also be the unwitting cause of this problem. If the gun is fired when just out of the shoulder the recoil characteristics are often not right to reset the mechanism, or the shooter may be failing to let go of the trigger between successive shots. The root of this problem is often more psychological than physical: you have to train your brain to pull the trigger, let go and then pull again, rather than pull and then try to pull the trigger further back. Some shooters experience enormous problems with this technique, while for others it never happens to them at all. If it does happen, only practice will eradicate a bad shooting habit.

Any failure to 'click' when the trigger is pulled must always be treated seriously and the gun must be assumed to be loaded and cocked. It must be unloaded immediately, and kept pointed in a safe direction while this is done.

Cartridges

Before we leave 'failure to fire' problems it is appropriate to look at what happens if a cartridge goes off outside a barrel, as could happen with a hang-fire. The real danger point is if it goes off inside the barrel with the breech open or partly open since in these conditions it may develop something close to full pressure and spray a lot of fragments around.

In fact, a cartridge going off outside a barrel, for any reason, is a rare occurrence. Generally cartridges may be dropped without danger, and the amount of heat required to set them off would normally be encountered only in a fire.

Should a cartridge go off outside a barrel the explosion will not as forceful as you might think.

The fact is that nitrocellulose normally burns relatively slowly when one considers what it is designed to do. To develop full pressure in a few milliseconds requires that a pretty sharp pressure curve must develop, and this generally happens only inside a barrel. The powder grains which are directly affected by the primer burn first and the pressure and heat that they build up set off the rest of the charge.

If these first grains start to burn outside the barrel their pressure tends to split the case or open the crimp. Denied pressure, the rest of the charge burns with a sharp fizz rather than a bang, and tends to release such pressure as there is into the atmosphere rather than use it to drive the shot forward.

Some years ago there were experiments in the USA to determine the dangers of cartridges going off outside barrels. One experimenter placed a cartridge inside a corrugated cardboard box of the type you might get from the supermarket and fired its primer by electrical means. The slight pressure generated was enough to raise the box lid, but all the cartridge's components were found within the box and none had penetrated the box walls. The experimenter then repeated the test with a bundle of cartridges to see whether all would go off if one were fired. Only the single cartridge attached to the electrodes went off and the results in terms of an explosion were equally disappointing.

I must confess to having felt a bit sceptical when I read a report of these tests in an American magazine and I was thinking of rigging up a similar experiment myself when I had a telephone call from a *Sporting Gun* reader. He had been out game shooting and had dropped a cartridge, base first, on to a gravel track. By coincidence, the primer had landed on the point of a piece of sharp flint and had gone off. The man, who was wearing normal outdoor winter clothing, suffered no injury whatever despite the fact that the cartridge had exploded only inches from his feet. He recalled hearing a 'phut' rather than

a bang and said that all the cartridge components were easily collected from within an area of a few square feet.

This, of course, does not mean that you can safely play games with cartridges, and ammunition should always be treated with respect. Primers are particularly dangerous, and setting them off outside a barrel liberates a lot of hot sparks and metal fragments. They also go off with an horrendous bang, as I once discovered to my cost. The exercise was to photograph a primer going off to illustrate a magazine article, and I set up what I thought was a safe test rig in my workshop. I was to take the picture in total darkness, lighting it with the flash of the primer firing. Apart from taking the precaution of firing the primer by using a mechanism attached to a long lanyard, I was also wearing a thick cotton boiler suit, a safety visor and earmuffs. What I heard as a dull thud was a bang so loud that it brought my neighbour round to find out what had exploded and, when I'd calmed him down, the third shot set fire to the background paper. I got my picture, but I would not do it again and I would not advise anyone, ever, to play with primers. It is not worth the risk.

Miscellaneous Ailments

There are, of course, other problems which are nothing to do with a failure to fire. Sometimes a gun will not open fully to allow you to insert a cartridge, and sometimes a gun seems to be spring-loaded for the last bit of its opening arc, forcing you to hold it open with one hand while you load it with the other. This is usually due to mechanical wear and tear – often to the sears – and if it does happen a gunsmith should be consulted right away. The problem is sometimes, but not always, associated with light trigger pulls.

A gun that will not close may be another problem for which there are many causes: a broken or a jammed bolt or bolt spring, or some other upset within the mechanism. But do beware: I once momentarily thought that my favourite game gun had let me down in this way, only to find that I was trying to close it with a fallen beechnut jammed in the mechanism!

EJECTOR PROBLEMS

One of the most annoying ejector problems is caused by the head of a spent cartridge slipping underneath the ejector, leaving you with a gun which can be neither closed nor fired. Sometimes you can wriggle the case out with a small screwdriver or, if the cartridge has a very shallow brass head, you can sometimes cut the metal part off with a penknife. However, you should not use any undue force or you might break the ejector leg. The safest way is to remove the ejector, if you know how, and replace it once the offending case has been withdrawn. Causes? A cartridge with an abnormally small head or a very rounded rim may be to blame. Usually, however, it is the ejector which is either worn or, particularly on an O/U shotgun, has become splayed outwards. The safest cure is to replace the ejector, if spares are available. If they are not, then a gunsmith may be able to bend the ejector back into its original profile. However, the risk of breakage may be relatively high depending upon the design and the composition of the steel, so let the gunsmith do it. If it then breaks, it's his fault; if you break it, it's yours.

Another intermittent fault on some guns may be that, if one cartridge has been fired and the gun is broken, both the fired case and the unfired cartridge are ejected together. The usual cause is a bent or jammed ejector rod, but it could also be a fault in the ejector kicker mechanism. Incidentally, when both cartridges have been fired, both cases should be ejected together, not one after the other.

KNOCKS AND BANGS

Any gun which has been dropped or banged against a solid object must be examined for barrel dents before it is fired again. A dent may cause a barrel to burst on the next shot, and even if it does not there could be unseen damage. An old chap once told me that he had dented his gun, fired a shot and the dent had miraculously come out to leave the barrels as good as new. Don't believe such nonsense: the dent may appear to have come out but the chances are that the following shot rearranged the metal in the barrel in such a way that there was a thin patch where the dent was, and that would be more dangerous than a dent, because it would not be so easily spotted.

Barrel dents are sometimes picked up when guns clang against the tubular metal edges of cages on sporting courses. Shooters sometimes get carried away and swing too far. If you have a club sporting course, a cheap way of preventing this problem is to cover the tubes with plastic pipe lagging secured with cable ties. But paint the cage with really good paint first, because the spongy lagging absorbs water and can promote rust on thinly painted steel.

MORE ON TRIGGERS

Triggers should fire with a pull of about 4lb, and anything below 3lb is potentially dangerous. Triggers that go 'light' usually have worn or rounded sears, which should be recut by a gunsmith. The job requires a lot of skill, and stoning sears to 'improve' trigger pulls can be particularly dangerous. It may leave trigger pulls which are erratic, dangerously light or even heavier and more 'creepy' than before you started.

AND, FINALLY...

As I complete this chapter it is the beginning of a November evening and a huge flight of over a thousand grey geese has just passed over my house, skilfully riding the gale on the tail end of a deep Atlantic depression to make their way along the Moray coast. Time to get out the 'fowling gun!

They bring with them a timely reminder that

guns used in hard conditions and often exposed to salt air suffer more from corrosion than do other guns. These guns need more than a cursory wipe on the outside before being put away, because rust can eat into hidden places and cause weaknesses which may soon be found by powerful goose shells. Do clean 'fowling guns carefully and stay safe.

Any gun which has a mechanical problem or is badly corroded is potentially dangerous. I know it is easy to preach, but don't say, 'Oh, I'll get it fixed sometime.' Get it fixed now! British shooting has the best safety record in the world and we should all work hard to maintain that reputation.

9 GUN SECURITY

THOSE WERE THE DAYS...

When I was a lad you could leave shotguns propped in the corner of the hall, although it was obviously unwise if there were children around. Then, with the general rise in crime, most of us started to keep guns out of sight. The Firearms (Amendment) Act of 1987, the legislation which followed the Hungerford massacre, obliged us to keep guns in safe places. Unfortunately, the Act did not define what a safe place was, and left the definition to Britain's fifty-two police forces, many of whom seemed to have different ideas. Some allowed guns to be kept in ordinary cupboards, provided they were secured with a chain or cable passed through the trigger guard, with a padlock.

Some even allowed guns to be kept in places of concealment, such as under floorboards and in obscure corners of lofts, but the consensus of police opinion was that shotguns should be kept in properly designed steel cabinets, secured to a structural wall of a building and closed with two good quality locks. The requirement annoyed many shooters at the time, but in many ways it made sense: guns held under such conditions could not be stolen in the course of the average break-in and were safe from not just children but inquisitive guests, the minority of dishonest tradesmen and other undesirables who find their way into respectable homes from time to time.

The situation was still far from clear. There being no formulated specification for a cabinet, there was still some disparity in the differing requirements of the police forces. Added to that, some forces were looking at the general level of home security as well, particularly in urban areas. Again, some shooters became annoyed and it is true that a few police officers were over-zealous on the general security requirement, calling for measures which were unnecessary and impracticable. However, efficient home security makes obvious good sense in that most of us have valuables other than guns we wish to safeguard and, while deliberate gun thefts are comparatively rare, general break-ins are all too common in some areas. It is likewise true that someone who breaks in with the intention of stealing your hi-fi equipment may also be tempted if he stumbles across an unsecured shotgun, even if he has no immediate intention of using it in crime. He may eventually pass it on to someone who has.

CABINET SPECIFICATION

The issue of cabinet specifications was generally solved by the publication of British Standard No. 7558, 1992, which required cabinets to be made of steel plate at least 2mm thick and also laid down minimum lock specifications and other common-sense security provisions. I say generally solved only because there was no statutory requirement for police forces to accept the British Standard, but, in practice, I have never heard of a BS7558 cabinet being rejected. On the other hand, I have heard of the Standard being accepted as the only standard, and there was a case of a man being refused permission to keep a gun in a very sophisticated Chubb security safe because it had only one lock! Then again, one police force allowed a chap to keep his gun in a disused condom vending machine because it fulfilled all the security criteria: the

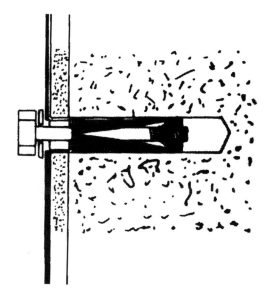

Method of attaching a cabinet to a wall with expansion bolts. The hole should be bored through the plaster, right into the masonry beneath. When the bolt it tightened a wedging action forces its sleeve to expand and jam tightly in the hole.

Gun security cabinets like this are available from most good gun shops.

steel was thick enough, it had a jemmy-resistant design, two locks and was bolted to a wall. You never can tell...

CABINET INSTALLATION

Now let us have a look at the business of cabinet fitting, starting from the beginning. The first job is to choose a site. You are not normally allowed to keep a gun in a garage or outbuilding, and there is the danger of rust in such places in any case. Hallways are always discouraged

because the cabinet is on view to casual visitors – it almost announces a gun's presence to any caller. Bedrooms and storage areas such as the cupboard under the stairs are favourite places and areas inside fitted wardrobes are good, too. Lofts are usually acceptable but should be used only if they are very dry, and any location should be well away from kitchen and bathroom steam. My cabinets are out of sight, inside a big store cupboard, so a burglar has first to break into the cupboard before he finds the cabinet and the working space inside is so tiny that it would give him an additional problem. If you cannot find such a location, then put the cabinet in a room corner if you can: it halves the possible angles of attack by a determined thief and may also provide you with an opportunity to bolt it to two walls instead of one.

Any location should back on to a solid wall made of brick, stone or building blocks to which the cabinet must be attached with expansion bolts, not wood screws and plugs, they are just not strong enough. Partition walls made of plasterboard, wood or old lath and plaster are no good either because the fixings can be pulled out when very little force is applied to them. If there is just nowhere in your house which meets these criteria, then lay the cabinet flat on its back on the floor, against a wall, and attach it to the floor joists with big coach screws; these are like giant woodscrews with square or hexagonal heads which have to be turned with a spanner. Do not use ordinary wood screws and do not attach the cabinet just to the floorboards – go right through into solid joists, the positions of which may usually be identified by a row of nails in the floorboards. Cabinets so fitted may often be disguised by covering them with dummy pipe trunking or in some other manner that makes them look like a part of the central heating system.

Before you decide on a location, probe the walls carefully and find out just where the real structural strength lies. Some walls have a layer of plasterboard with a gap behind them and in this case you may need very long mounting bolts. In some old houses, such as mine, nooks beside chimney breasts have been boarded over and what look like solid walls are just thin layers of board with up to 18in of air space behind them. In such a place you may consider cutting through the board, mounting the cabinet against the wall and putting a dummy cupboard door in front of it.

When you bring your cabinet from the gun shop take a friend with you. Cabinets are heavy, and particularly difficult to lift into cars, up stairs and round awkward corners. You will also need to call at the hardware store or DIY shop and buy four $^3/_8$in or 8mm expansion bolts, and the recommended masonry drill if you do not have one already.

Once the cabinet is in position you can press it against the wall, open the door and find the predrilled mounting holes. Mark the hole centres on the wall with a pencil or ballpoint pen, take the cabinet away and drill the holes, taking precautions against dust if you value your home life! Then poke the outer sheaths of the expansion bolts down the holes. With the cabinet back in position, you can then pass the bolts through the predrilled holes and tighten them. If you are mounting on to brick or stone you can use quite a lot of torque, but some building blocks are rather crumbly so you will have to use your judgement here. In any case, the cabinet should be so solid that it does not move when you push it to the limit of your strength, and you should be confident that it cannot be levered off with common tools. If the building blocks are very friable it may be necessary to cement the bolts in; there are also some very expensive bolts which cement themselves fast with a built-in tube of epoxy resin which is released when they are tightened.

Skirting boards may be a curse because they prevent the base of the cabinet from fitting flush against the wall. If this is the case either cut away a section of the skirting or mount the cabinet with solid timber blocks underneath it so that it is high enough to clear the obstruction.

Against an open wall you may also consider building some sort of wooden cupboard around your cabinet. This disguise gives a little extra security and also hides from view what is likely to be a rather ugly structure, if it is in a room you often use. If you have plenty of money to spend you can also buy cabinets which come ready disguised as pieces of antique furniture.

It is usual for cabinets to be supplied with two or three sets of keys. You can put one set with your house keys, so that they are always with you when you go out, and find a really secure hiding place for the spares. Do not go for obvious places such as inside ornaments: find somewhere really obscure or remote. I used to keep my spares in a security cupboard at my office, which was 20 miles from where I live; but now I work from home I've had to find another hiding place. Fortunately, in an old house there are plenty of nooks and crannies, and it would take a burglar a great deal of time to search them all.

HOUSE SECURITY

Now let us look at the house itself. I once sought

police advice on this, and the first thing their security adviser said was, 'Well, how would you get in if you had lost your key? If it's easy for you, it's easy for a burglar.'

Some easy steps are obvious and cost nothing: you should not leave spare keys under stones, hanging on nails in out-houses or dangling on bits of string down drainpipes, because these are the first places the criminal tends to examine. You also lock away ladders, steps or anything else which might be used as climbing equipment, and lop the branches of trees which might provide access to upper windows or rooftops. Sheds containing carpentry and engineering tools, tyre levers or anything else which might aid a housebreaker should be locked.

You then take off the toy locks which are provided by some house builders and fit Chubbs or some other reputable models which are not easily picked and which will stand up to a shoulder-charge by a heavy man. Also pay attention to the door frame: no lock, no matter how strong and sophisticated, is much good if its tongue engages with a slot in flimsy timber. You also fit good, strong bolts to the top and the bottom of every door and make sure the doors are hung on strong hinges. No locks or bolts of any quality will help you much if the hinges will yield to a good, hefty kick, and three hinges are always better than two. Chain bolts are a good idea, too, particularly if you live alone or if members of your family are often in your house alone while you are away. You also fit window locks downstairs and to upstairs windows to which there might be access via drainpipes or low roofs. If a window is never opened and is not part of a fire escape route, you can drive a couple of heavy wood screws through the frame, a cheap and easy solution.

Note that these are just sensible precautions for any house, not just those containing guns. The police are entitled to expect a sensible level of security, in keeping with the area in which you live; but they should not demand that you turn your house into a suburban Fort Knox.

For your own peace of mind you might also think about security lights with passive infra-red switches. They can be a nuisance in that they are sometimes switched on by passing cats, dogs or other creatures; or just by the natural movement of trees on some days, but a few hundred watts of light do much to deter intruders. The occasional false alarm is a small price to pay and lights which come on for no apparent reason are likely to deter anyone watching your house.

Of course, you can't always win. Some years back, I did all these things to my old house in Lincolnshire. I even joined the local Neighbourhood Watch. The burglar, when he came, struck in daylight and used the bright yellow Neighbourhood Watch sticker on the kitchen window as an aiming mark for his brick. He stole my great-grandfather's gold watch, but he didn't get at my guns.

If you own several guns or have particular valuables in your house then you may wish to consider a proper, electronic security system. If you think that you need one, consult the experts and spend a sensible amount of money. The presence of a dummy alarm box on the outside of the house may be a mixed blessing: it may deter, but it is also an indication that there is something inside worth stealing, and the fact that it is a dummy may be easily spotted by an experienced thief. You hear horror stories about cowboy alarm fitters, so spend your money with a reputable firm, and make sure that the system is sufficiently simple for all the members of the family to be able to set and disarm it: in that way it gets set every time someone leaves the house. And do not, like someone I know, use your telephone number as the key code which disarms it...

CARTRIDGES

Currently there is no security requirement for shotgun cartridges, but it makes good sense to keep them out of the reach of children and in a place where they are not on view to casual visitors. They are best kept at room temperature, because extremes of cold affect their perform-

A hard case like this offers a gun the best of protection, but it is impracticable in the field.

ance. They should also be kept dry. A lockable cupboard inside the house is highly worthwhile.

GUNS IN CARS

While your gun is in transit you are expected to take 'reasonable care' that it is not stolen. You are allowed to leave it in a locked car for a few minutes while you go into a shop to make a purchase, but it should be concealed in a locked boot rather than be on view on the back seat. It must be contained within a slip or carrying box while it is in your car or being carried in a public place. If you have an estate car you can cover the slip with a blanket or coat.

A great deal of car security boils down to common sense. If you leave your car in an area where car theft is common, then it is clearly unwise to leave your gun in it. You may also attract potential thieves by displaying stickers proclaiming loyalty to particular brands of gun, shooting equipment or shooting magazines.

And, as well as concealing your gun, it is also wise to conceal anything else which could give a clue to its presence such as cartridge boxes, skeet vests or hearing protectors.

If you are particularly worried you can bolt a secure carrying box into the boot of your car or pass a length of steel cable down inside your gun slip, through the trigger guard and lock it to some part of the car's structure. Car boots usually contain hollow structures through which cables can be passed. Additionally, taking the fore-end off and putting it in your pocket at least means that the gun could not be fired if it were stolen. This, of course, does not prevent the car itself from being stolen, complete with gun. It has to be said that the majority of cars are not very secure against theft and that few people take much notice of car alarms any more. Dogs, however, are rated as a good deterrent to theft.

All these things considered, it is clearly unwise to leave guns in unattended cars for more than a few minutes, and not at all in some areas. Let common sense prevail!

10 SIMPLE TOOLS AND PROCEDURES

Victorian engineers had great skills in building machines of enormous mechanical complexity. The only way in which they could make their creations perform as they wished was to use a multiplicity of metal parts to transmit motion from its source to the place where it could do useful work and, in the better examples, 'fail safe' if something went wrong. Machines now tend to be simpler, and electronics are employed to perform the complex functions.

The shotgun as we know it today was designed by Victorians and it is therefore a purely mechanical device. Fortunately, the business of locking a gun closed by mechanical means and causing a hammer to fall on a firing pin when a trigger is pulled is not that difficult, yet the average shotgun still has around seventy separate parts which must work in harmony and fit together with great precision.

SCREWS

The mechanism of most guns is held together with simple screws and pins, and gunsmiths confuse the issue by traditionally calling screws

A screwdriver with a blade ground to this profile may easily jump out of the slots in gun screws and cause damage.

Never use an electric screwdriver on guns. However, the blade profile is excellent and can be copied on your hand tools.

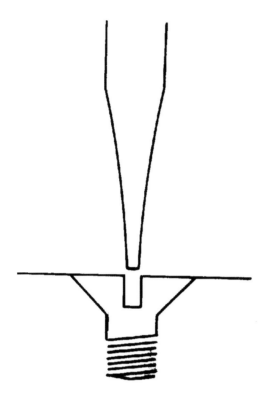

A screwdriver ground to this profile tends not to jump out of the slot in the screw head and cause damage.

pins, while pins are referred to as pegs. By a further strange quirk of tradition, a gunsmith refers to a screwdriver as a turnscrew. Surely, if there were any true consistency a screwdriver should be a 'turnpin'.

Be that as it may, guns are relatively simple to take to pieces with everyday tools. The average modern O/U or semi-auto can be disassembled with a selection of screwdrivers, a few pin punches and a small hammer no heavier than 4oz. Screwdrivers, however, frequently need to be ground to a different profile from those used in other trades.

The screws in guns are usually made with very thin screwdriver slots, which helps them to look more elegant. It also makes them easy to damage if they are not removed with the proper tools: heads may become chipped and burred and the appearance of the gun is spoiled for want of a little care and preparation.

A screwdriver should fill as much of the width of the screw slot as possible, and it should also seat right down to the bottom of the slot so that the required amount of torque may be applied without damage. It is therefore usual not only to thin down the blade tips of screwdrivers to be used on guns, but also to grind them to a hollow profile. On some tools this can be done quite easily with a round or half-round file, while others are so hard they need to be taken to a grinding wheel where great care has to be taken not to overheat and soften the blades. The secret is to take off a very little at a time, and stop if you see the blade change colour. It is quite usual practice in a gun shop to file or grind a screwdriver to a suitable profile for an individual screw if there is not already one on the rack to do the job.

The easy way around this requirement is to buy a set of gunmaker's turnscrews, but they are expensive. If you have the ability to reprofile the blades, it is much cheaper to buy your screwdrivers from normal tool outlets or DIY shops. If you want to do serious work on your gun then you may need several screwdrivers tailored to its individual requirements. Remember that nothing looks worse than a nice gun with burred and chipped screw heads, and no one will want to buy a gun so damaged.

REMOVING THE STOCK

Most gun work other than routine cleaning also involves the removal of the stock. The stocks on most modern O/Us – and some side-by-sides – are held on by a single bolt which is found at the bottom of a long hole drilled through from the butt end, the tip of which engages with a female thread in the back of the action. These stock drawbolts usually have hexagonal heads (commonly between 10 and 14mm across the flats); but they also often have a screwdriver slot cut in the head. If you remove these bolts with screwdrivers you need to take great care that the blade tip is located firmly in the slot before you apply any torque. It is very easy to get an impression that the blade is correctly located and then find out the hard way that it is not. If the blade is wedged down the side of the bolt head and torque is applied, the forces are often sufficient to crack the stock. In fact, it is not unknown for screwdrivers to break through the walls of very slim stocks.

If, like me, you take off a lot of stocks, then it is a good idea to build a special stock-bolt screwdriver like the one in the picture. Note that the protruding blade is just deep enough to penetrate the slot and that the body is so fat that it automatically aligns the blade with the axis of the hole. This blade cannot do any damage.

The other way is to use a socket spanner on a long extension. Bolt heads are commonly 10, 12 or 14mm across the flats, and the familiar $1/_2$in drive sockets used in engineering and for work on cars are sometimes too fat to go down the hole. A $3/_8$in drive set, on which the sockets are usually thinner in the wall, is a better bet.

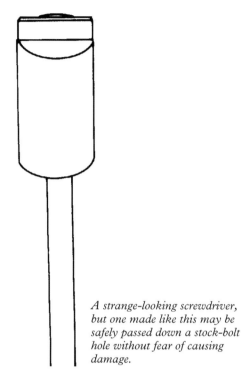

A strange-looking screwdriver, but one made like this may be safely passed down a stock-bolt hole without fear of causing damage.

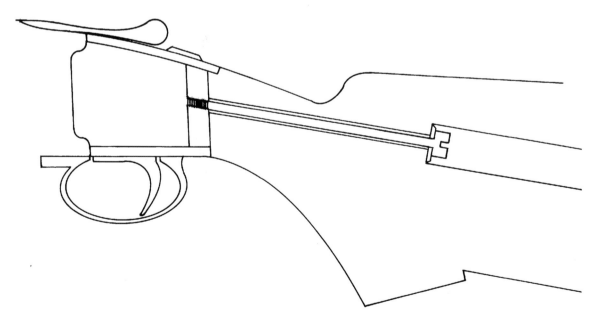

How the woodwork is attached to the action by a hidden draw bolt at the bottom of a long hole in the stock wood.

Otherwise for a cheap solution you can buy a cheap tubular spanner and braze on an extension made from $^3/_8$in or 10mm round steel rod with a 'T' piece at the other end. You can even just bend a few inches of the end over at a right angle, anything that will allow you to apply the necessary torque to loosen the bolt.

Some guns (notably Berettas and Classic Doubles) use a socket-head screw in this location. That on the Beretta has a 6mm head, while the Classic Doubles head and some others are 5mm. Not all guns are provided with keys, and the best alternative is an Allen key tip on your socket set.

Once the buttplate has been removed the stock bolt hole is easily visible.

When taking the stock off some guns the wood screw in the tang of the trigger guard has to be removed first.

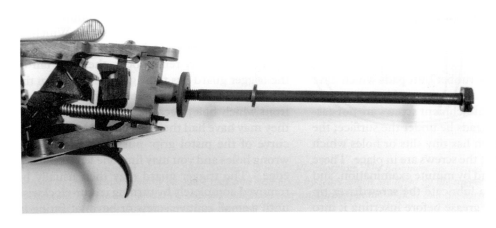

This is the position of the stock bolt in most designs of O/U shotguns. It should not be over-tightened.

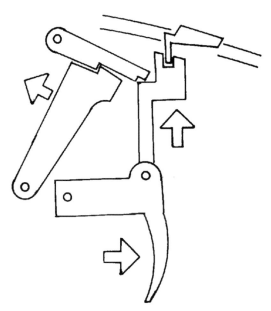

The trigger and safety mechanisms taken in isolation. In this case the gun is ready to fire, and when the trigger is pulled the sear will be lifted, allowing the hammer to move forward under the spring pressure.

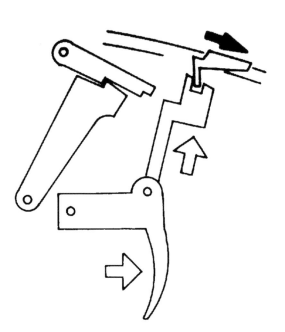

If the safety catch is pulled back the trigger mechanism is disconnected from the sear, so that if the trigger is pulled the sear cannot be lifted.

do keep the parts in a tin or a box rather than allow them to lie loose on your bench top; if it helps, take notes as you work so that you do not have to commit the reassembly order to memory.

The best surface on which to work is a wooden-topped bench or a firm wooden table, and great care should be taken if gun parts have to be gripped in a vice. The normal, serrated vice jaws should be covered with either wood, a soft metal such as copper, aluminium or lead, or a suitable, non-brittle plastic. Barrels should never be gripped across the diameter of the bore: the only safe way is to grip them by the lumps. If gripped in any other way they may be squashed out of round: remember that with an ordinary engineer's vice it is possible to apply a gripping pressure of around four tons.

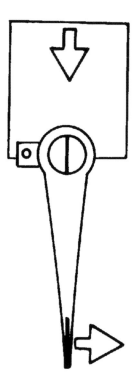

Looking down on the top lever. When the lever is pressed to the right against a spring a crank or cam mechanism pulls the bolt backwards.

By and large, you can disassemble whatever you like, but do not compromise your own safety and that of your fellow shooters. Botched repairs are always potentially dangerous, and it is also very unwise to try to regulate triggers – they are best left to the experts.

BLACKING

Much amateur gunsmithing concerns work on the cosmetic appearance of guns, and this often involves minor repairs to the blacking. Most gun shops sell blacking or blueing compounds, and I have heard some scary stories regarding their use in recent years. It is not that there is anything wrong with the products, but manufacturers now use a wide variety of chemical blacking recipes, and they are not all compatible with one another.

One *Sporting Gun* reader who called me with a problem had slightly damaged the surface of the action of a Browning Gti. The action on these guns is finished in a very deep black, and after he had polished out the scratch he applied a commercial gun-blacking compound to the

The inner workings of this gun – a Winchester – are typical of the modern breed of O/U shotguns. Note the powerful main springs, running on guide rods.

Close-up of a sear mechanism. Note that there is a very small area of contact.

This is what goes on inside the fore-end of a gun with ejectors which are not spring-loaded. Coil springs power the two kickers which work the mechanism.

area. It certainly blacked the bare bit, but it also removed the original blacking from the surrounding area. After that, the only suggestion I now make is that all blacking compounds should first be tried on a hidden portion of the gun, where it is possible to check that they are not going to react badly with any existing surface finish. A tiny experiment that has gone wrong in an area hidden by the fore-end wood is not going to be noticed; an ugly splodge further forward on the barrel certainly is.

This procedure is always wise because, even if there is no bad reaction, there are, strange as it may seem, many different shades and textures of black. Some are bluish and shiny, while others are deep and soft matt, with every possible variation in between. A repair with the wrong shade or texture often looks worse than the original damage: remember how badly stains show up on a black sweater.

This being the case, small components such as top levers and trigger guards are best completely cleaned down, polished and reblacked all over rather than just patched. They are at least then the same shade of black all over.

Each different type of blacking compound comes with its own instructions, but all require the component first to be cleaned and then thor-

oughly degreased. Depending on the amount of surface damage, surface preparation can begin with quite a coarse abrasive – even a fine file if the damage is deep – and continue with increasingly fine grades of wet-and-dry abrasive paper until the required surface finish is achieved. If you have access to one, you may use a calico polishing wheel and a little jeweller's rouge for a final polish, but most of us have to work down through the grades of paper. A good final finish can often be achieved by vigorous rubbing with fine wet-and-dry lubricated with oil or diluted washing-up liquid.

Many of the old degreasing fluids we used to use, such as carbon tetrachloride, are now unavailable on health and safety grounds, and the traditional gunsmithing brew is a paste made of powdered chalk and water, which is brushed on, allowed to dry and then removed with a dry, clean brush. This works but it may be messy on a small scale, and some readily available solvents are quite effective. Cigarette lighter fluid is also quite good (although it is highly inflammable and gives off nasty fumes); after it has been rubbed off with a clean cotton cloth the component should not then be touched with the fingers. Fingers leave greasy prints and you may end up with a job bearing a permanent set of which they would be proud at the police station.

You then just follow the instructions on the product you have bought, but bearing in mind that most are quite poisonous and may damage your skin. They are usually creams which are rubbed on with a rag, or liquids in which the components may be immersed. Always be safe, and wear rubber or plastic gloves. Whatever the process, allow the substance to do its work, then carefully follow the instructions for 'killing' it. This 'killing' process is important, otherwise the component may rust very quickly. After it is finished an extra soak in warm, soapy water does no harm and ensures that the last vestiges of the chemical have been removed. After that, the newly blacked surface should be oiled and it is often best to leave it very oily for a few days. Remember that all of these substances are made for blacking steel; they will not work on brass or any other metal.

I have tried blacking complete barrel sets with these over-the-counter preparations, but the results have invariably been rather blotchy when they are closely examined. Large components such as these are usually best passed over to the gun trade for a professional job in a big tank. It is not expensive and you may be able to reduce the cost by doing the surface preparation yourself.

Very small components, such as screw heads, may be blacked with oil. You just heat the screw until it is black hot, immerse it in a suitable oil, return it to the flame to burn off the excess, and – when it has cooled – polish it. Motor oils do not work because they contain additives which prevent the formation of black ash when they become overheated. After much experimentation I have found that the best preparation to be melted Flora margarine. It leaves your work area smelling like a fire in a chip shop, but it works on most steels. The process is fine on the heads of wood screws used to secure things such as trigger guards and butt plates, but – because it may soften the steel – it should not be used on any screws or pins which come under stress when the gun is fired.

MORE ON SCREWS – STUCK

Screws which have become seized in their threads are a constant blight when one restores or repairs old guns. To really get a purchase on a screw, first find a screwdriver that fits exactly, then lay the gun down on a bench or table, preferably on a few layers of folded cloth or a thin cushion to stop it sliding about. Then lean over your work so that you can put a fair proportion of your body weight on to the screwdriver before you begin to turn it. In that way, the screwdriver will not jump out of the slot and burr its edges, or do worse damage to the engraving.

If the screw still does not yield, try giving it a light tap on the head with a blunt-ended punch and a small hammer, but do not use enough force to dent or bruise it if it is a screw unique to the gun. Some screws have specially shaped heads which can only be reproduced as one-offs on a lathe, and some have engraving patterns which are difficult to reproduce. If you use light blows on such screws it is best to use a piece of hard wood or very soft metal as a drift.

If a light tap on the head does not work, take the woodwork off the gun and heat the offending metal part as hot as you can get it on an ordinary, water-filled domestic radiator – no hotter – and give it a good soak in either penetrating oil or diesel. In this process, traditional, old English blacking may be at some risk, but at least it may free the screw. A soaking in Coca-Cola, surprisingly, has been known to work too.

– Loose

This is the opposite of the previous problem: screws which shoot loose as the gun is repeatedly fired. The screws which secure the fore-end wood to the iron are particular offenders on some O/Us. Sometimes all that is necessary is to clean the head and give it a tiny dab of fast-drying, clear varnish before it is tightened down; but a better result is achieved by taking out the screw, cleaning it and reinstating it with a tiny drop of Loctite on the thread. Be careful about the grade you buy – you need the soft-setting threadlocker, not the stuff that is used to make strong, engineering joints, otherwise you may never get the screw out again. Loctite has the peculiar property that it cures when deprived of air, which is how it manages to set in the tiny crevices within threads. Whatever you do, do not over-tighten screws which habitually shoot loose: you may snap off the heads and finish up in a worse pickle than before.

WHAT YOU MAY DO

There are few legal constraints on what you may do to your own shotgun. Even if you render it out of proof and potentially dangerous, that is counted as being your own fault and you have a legal problem only if you are unwise enough to offer the gun for sale in that condition. The law is designed to protect other people, not to save you from your own folly.

You may not shorten the barrel of a shotgun below 24in and continue to hold it on a Shotgun Certificate, as the law defines a shotgun as having a barrel of 2ft feet or longer in length and a shorter barrel means that the gun becomes a Section One Firearm subject to a Firearms Certificate. Such a certificate would be difficult to get, because it would be hard to show the justification for owning a gun with barrels so short. Only registered firearms dealers are allowed to shorten barrels to the degree required for resleeving. Neither may you increase the magazine capacity of a repeating shotgun beyond two cartridges, unless you have already been granted a Firearms Certificate to hold such a gun.

Beyond that, the only rules are those dictated by common sense. Think first, be safe, and never hesitate to seek professional advice.

11 CARTRIDGES

PROBLEMS IN THE PAST

Until the beginning of the nineteenth century every system of firearms ignition required fire to be struck outside the barrel, in the atmosphere, applied to powder in an external pan and from there conducted to the main charge inside the barrel via a touch hole. In practical terms the various systems had severe disadvantages for the shooter.

There were match locks, wheel locks and flint locks, and the reliability of all of them was constantly at the mercy of wind and weather. Powder in the pan could be dampened by rain and blown away by wind – and there was more. The system was slow: guns went off with a sort of 'click-fizz-bang', which was a distinct disadvantage for a shotgunner tackling a moving target. It called for a very long and steady swing, which had to be continued after the trigger had been pulled or the target would be missed behind. And for high overhead shots there was a further disadvantage: burning grains of powder from the pan could fall back into the shooter's face, which must have wrought havoc when luxuriant whiskers were much in fashion.

Added to all this was the fact that a muzzle-loader was very slow to reload, even with a prepared, paper cartridge containing powder, wad and shot. This was certainly no fun in the sporting field, but it must have brought a new dimension to fear for a soldier in an exposed position on a hillside, having to go through a long performance with a ramrod while under fire.

The development of the modern cartridge took place in two distinct phases: first came an improved, faster and more reliable ignition system, and then – with the invention of the breech-loading gun – came the cartridge as we know it today. It took more than a hundred years for all the components to come together.

BETTER SHOOTING THROUGH CHEMISTRY

The story began in the late 1700s, when the English chemist Edward Howard devised a safer method of making an already known explosive compound: fulminate of mercury. Early experimenters tried to use this substance to improve the power of gunpowder, often with alarming and dangerous results. One such experimenter was the Rev. Alexander James Forsyth, a Church of Scotland Minister from a parish near Aberdeen. He was a keen shooter who also had an interest in chemistry and, inevitably, one day an experiment went wrong and he blew up his workshop. The luckless cleric finished up, bruised and battered, outside in the street.

The experience caused him to abandon mercury fulminate as a propellant and concentrate on its use as an igniter for a main charge of gunpowder: he discovered that it would explode reliably if it was struck by a hard enough blow, and this was to be the key to the modern cartridge.

Forsyth's system contained the fulminate within a bottle-shaped attachment at the side of the gun's lock mechanism, and he tried to sell the idea to the government of the day. At first the military authorities showed great interest, but eventually sent him packing. They were, however, to use some of his ideas, and they finally got around to awarding him £1,000 for them – three months after his death in 1843.

The real future lay in the incorporation of the fulminate in a crushable, copper cap which, when fitted over a nipple screwed into the touch hole, could be struck by a hammer and thereby strike fire to the main charge. Its precise history is obscure, and claimants to its invention in the early 1800s include the London gunsmith Joseph Egg, Colonel Peter Hawker (a leading sportsman of the day), Joseph Manton (another gunmaker) and an artist named Joshua Shaw. A cap, well-seated on a nipple, was windproof and rainproof, did not shower the shooter with burning fragments, and did away with the need to prime a pan before a gun could be fired. The system was accepted by the military in 1838 and from then on became an increasingly common fitment on guns of all types, both military and sporting.

FURTHER DEVELOPMENTS

More than a century was to pass before the second phase of development fell into place, and credit for the first practical break-action, breech-loading shotgun goes to the Paris gun-

The primer sits in a cup pressed into the centre of the cartridge head.

maker Lefaucheau, who in 1850 produced a gun powered by a rimmed, gas-tight cartridge invented by a fellow Parisian, Houllier. The cartridge was a pin-fire, which contained a percussion cap in its base which was fired by a pin which projected vertically through a groove in the breech face and the breech end of the barrel. The cartridge fired when the pin was struck by an external hammer.

The centre-fire cartridge as we know it was introduced to England by George Daw in 1861 and from that day until this only details have been improved. We have new primer materials, new propellants, new case and wad materials, and improved closures, but Daw's cartridge would be immediately recognized for what it is – the father of the modern shotshell.

GOODBYE TO GUNPOWDER

First improvements came in the form of new powders to replace traditional gunpowder. Gunpowder had the advantage that, in the quantities in which it could be loaded into a shotgun cartridge, it burned relatively slowly to produce a reasonably low pressure which could be safely contained within a barrel made by traditional means from the metals available to nineteenth-century gunsmiths. Its disadvantages were that it burned with much evil-smelling smoke, it fouled barrels with corrosive residues which had to be laboriously scrubbed out as soon as possible after shooting, and the limits of its performance were being overtaken by improvements to steels and in methods of gun barrel manufacture.

Compared with other substances required to burn rapidly – petroleum, for instance – a gun propellant needs one unique property: as it burns it must produce its own oxygen to support combustion in the gas-tight confines of a cartridge. Old-fashioned black gunpowder does this and, from the middle of the last century onwards, the search was on to find another, more powerful propellant which would do the same thing yet burn with little smoke and leave

This is a typical disc propellant powder, greatly magnified.

a smaller quantity of corrosive residues. Power proved to be no problem: in fact, many substances provided too much of it too suddenly, with disastrous results. What was needed was reliable power which could be regulated by chemistry to burn at the right rate for sharp performance without the sudden generation of dangerous pressures.

The answer was found to be a compound called nitrocellulose, which began to become popular towards the end of the century. Early powders were produced by steeping sawdust in nitric acid, while their modern counterparts are produced by a process which begins by treating short strands of raw cotton with the same acid. Other chemicals and manufacturing methods are used to regulate the ignition qualities and burn rate, while the size and the shape of individual flakes have further influences on performance. In summary: thin flakes of large surface area burn faster than coarser lumps, and very fine powders burn fast too. Sometimes a little nitroglycerine is added to the mix, and these so-called 'double-base' powders generally have improved cold-weather performance.

Primers, originally powered by mercury fulminate and later by potassium chlorate,

remained a source of barrel corrosion until the introduction of modern primers based on lead styphnate, while cartridge cases progressed through several grades of paper with ever-increasing resistance to water, until the modern plastic case was introduced in the 1950s. Some of the older paper cases swelled so much when wet that they would not fit into the gun's chamber and, even if they did and could be fired satisfactorily, the case head often came off on extraction. This left the shooter with a length of cardboard-like tube firmly wedged in the chamber of his gun, which explains that hook-like object often found among vintage shooting equipment.

THE CRIMPED CLOSURE

Ballistic problems were defeated one by one, and a significant development was that of the crimped closure. Most cartridges, until after the Second World War, had a cardboard disc placed on top of the shot and were closed by the rim of the case being rolled over it in a ring. When this rolled turnover came undone, as pressure in the cartridge increased sharply at the moment of

The most usual way of sealing a cartridge is with a crimp closure like this.

This rolled turnover incorporates what is known as a frangible disc – a disc of hard plastic which shatters and breaks up when the shot is fired.

firing, it released the cardboard disc which travelled ahead of the shot column right through the barrel. Once in the atmosphere the disc, being light and presented to the atmosphere flat-on, decelerated rapidly, often diverting individual shot pellets from their true path. The answer was to get rid of the card disc and close the cartridge by folding the end of the case material in a star pattern – the so-called crimp closure. In modern cartridges there is usually enough case material to form this type of closure when all components have been loaded; but in loads which are so bulky that the old rolled turnover has to be used most modern loaders use an over-shot disc of brittle plastic, known as a frangible disc, which shatters at the moment of firing and therefore does not disturb the shot pattern as it develops outside the muzzle.

THE WADDING COLUMN

The wadding column is another component which has much influence on the ballistic performance of the cartridge. Early wads, usually of greased felt, served no other purpose than to form – it was hoped – a gas-tight seal between the burning powder and the shot, and thus both increase the velocity of the charge and save shot pellets from damage by an expanding volume of extremely hot gas. The principle remained the same until the 1950s when the plastic cup-type wad was introduced.

This new wad did much to improve cartridge performance on several fronts. First, its base could be made like a small, inverted cup. This gave an excellent gas seal without resorting to the extremes of interference fit in the barrel which had been common with felt or fibre wads. Secondly, the plastic wad incorporated a gradually collapsing latticework section above the base which gave the shot charge a slightly more gradual acceleration and thereby saved the lower pellets in the stack from crushing damage, which forced them out of round and therefore caused erratic flight. And, thirdly and most important, being enclosed in a cup, the shot was

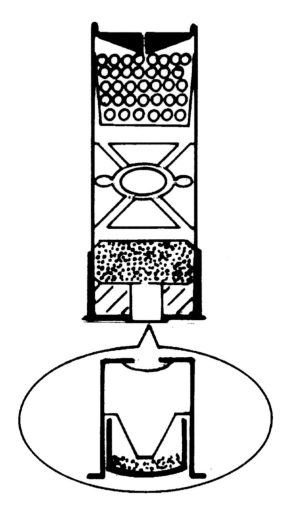

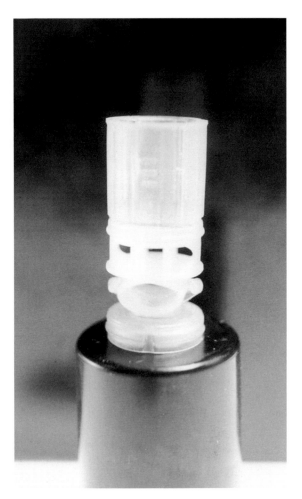

Cross-section of a plastic-wad cartridge. The shot sits in its cup, under the crimp. Beneath that is the compression area of the wad, with the powder beneath that. A small amount of priming material is held in the base of the primer. When this cup is indented, the compound is crushed against the anvil and bursts into flame.

The wad in a plastic-wad cartridge forms a cup which prevents contact and friction between the pellets and the barrel walls.

no longer subject to great friction as it passed along the barrel and through the choke. So, again, it was saved from damage and therefore emerged into the atmosphere in a truly round state capable of stable flight.

All these factors combined to improve velocities and patterns enormously – with one penalty. Whereas felt and fibre degraded quite rapidly once on the ground, under the influence of rain and dew, plastic remains undegraded, possibly for hundreds of years. Not only are white plastic wads unsightly (albeit in extremely small numbers when the total land area is considered), but they are also a hazard to grazing farm stock, which are likely to swallow them and suffer consequential intestinal blockages. It is therefore normal, and good practice, to use fibre wads for all shots which are likely to fall on grazing land. For general countryside shooting, most manufacturers now make cartridges with

Components of a fibre-wad cartridge (Winchester). The wad is in two pieces, which is not unusual, but the cup-shaped card which sits beneath it is a Winchester speciality.

Typical components of a plastic-wad cartridge. This particular wad is a photodegradable component by Gualandi of Italy.

These components of a fibre wadding column are usually a considerable interference fit in the barrel.

photodegradable plastic wads, which break down in a matter of months under the influence of ultra-violet light. However, at present the wads do not degrade fast enough to be used over grazing land and so the traditional fibre wad still has its place in shooting.

THE SHOT

From the earliest times shot has been made by dropping molten lead from the top of a tall tower through a wire gauze to provide droplets of the desired size. Molten lead has the property that, as it falls through the atmosphere, it forms into perfectly spherical pellets rather than the teardrop shapes formed by most other falling liquids. At the bottom of the tower the pellets, already cooled by their fall through the air, drop into a tub of water, which further cools them and decelerates them without damage. The tower method is still employed, although many modern shot plants now use a short-drop technique perfected in Germany. On the short-drop Bleimeister machine, pellets fall into water from a height of only a few inches, and form into true spheres as they roll down a submerged incline.

Good shot appears bright, well-polished and perfectly round.

The dimensional accuracy of shot may be checked with an ordinary engineer's micrometer.

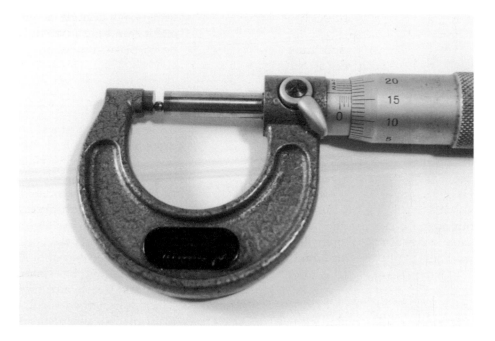

Pure lead is rather too soft for shotgun pellets: it distorts under the pressure of firing, forcing pellets to go out of round, and the pressure may also cause individual pellets to cold-weld together into irregular lumps which do not fly true and which present considerable danger because of their increased mass and range. This may be prevented by the addition of a little antimony to the mix (usually no more than 4 per cent), which hardens the pellets.

The hardness of lead pellets is usually expressed as a percentage 'crush value', derived by first measuring the diameter of a pellet and then measuring it again after it has had a $\frac{1}{2}$lb steel weight dropped on it from a height of 3in, after which the percentage of crush can be worked out. Most competition shot provides values of 30 per cent or less, harder lead producing even lower values. Some game shot is a little softer (up to 35 per cent) and is deliberately made with these values so that it distorts slightly once inside the bird and thereby dissipates its energy without passing right through. Note that the test provides a good idea of hardness but is not exact in engineering terms. It also goes considerably 'off-scale' on pellets bigger than size 6 or smaller than 7 $\frac{1}{2}$, big pellets producing artificially low figures while small pellets may appear to be extremely soft.

Most shot is polished and lubricated by tumbling it in a dry lubricant such as graphite. This further helps to prevent cold-welding and also inhibits damage as it passes through the constrictions of a choke. Superior lubrication may be achieved by plating the shot with metals such as copper, nickel or brass. This plating, contrary to popular belief, is for lubrication purposes only and does not enhance the hardness of the pellets. The plating of pellets is an expensive process, so plated shot is usually only found in top-quality loads.

LEAD SUBSTITUTES

At the time of writing there is world-wide pressure to remove lead from the environment because of its toxic nature. At present there is a voluntary ban on the use of lead shot over wetlands, where there is a possibility that spent pellets may be ingested by waterfowl. Some European countries have legislated against lead shot, while in the USA substitutes have to be used for waterfowl shooting.

The most common substitute for lead is soft iron, known to shooters as 'steel shot'. Being lighter than lead (it has a specific gravity of around 7, compared with 11 for lead), it is less efficient down-range. It may also damage guns when it is fired through tight chokes and is the subject of special proof requirements introduced by the Commission International Permanente (CIP), the international organization of proof houses. Currently we have an international standard for guns required to fire steel shot, but no guns tested to the new specification – a situation we can only hope will be clarified in the near future. In the meantime, the only safe course when using steel is to obey the instructions on the ammunition packet to the absolute letter.

It is also doubly important that steel-loaded cartridges are not allowed to get damp, otherwise pellets may rust together and form a solid projectile which would ruin a barrel and probably blow up the gun.

Other, more suitable, substitutes are under development. Eley have had success by substituting another heavy metal, bismuth, for lead, and it shows great promise although it is rather expensive. Other loaders are using zinc and tin, and all these metals, to the best of current knowledge, are non-damaging to guns. However, all are lighter than lead so all suffer a lower down-range performance, although down-range bismuth comes very close to lead. Bismuth can be used in the familiar lead shot sizes, but with other metals this lack of mass is compensated for by loading cartridges with fewer, larger pellets and driving them as fast as possible within the limits of safe chamber pressures.

There have also been a number of attempts to produce non-lead shot by incorporating particles of very heavy metals such as tungsten and molybdenum within a plastic matrix. Such pellets are extremely expensive to produce and to date none has been a commercial success.

CHOICE OF CARTRIDGE

Accepting that the gun is in proof, a 12-bore cartridge choice is first dictated by the length of the gun's chambers. There are still a few old

Two excellent shotgun cartridges for field shooting: Winchester's GB Classic and Hull's Sterling Game.

These are the largest and the smallest cartridge in common use – a 20-bore (left) and a 12-bore, 3in, magnum (right)

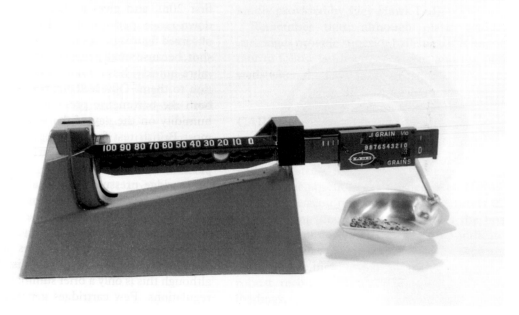

A simple powder scale like this, accurate to around 0.1 of a grain, is a valuable tool for checking cartridge loading.

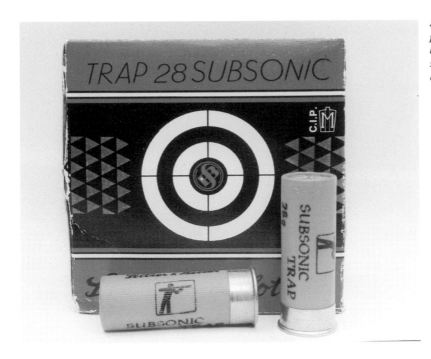

Subsonic cartridges, of very low power, are useful for training lightly built people or on shooting grounds where there is a noise problem.

of 1,400ft/sec, an observed figure of around 1,070ft/sec and a pressure of 550 bars. The only area in which to be generally wary is when choosing wildfowling cartridges which may be advertised as semi-magnums. Pressures are usually high, to the point that some, although loaded in 70mm cases, are best shot through magnum-proofed guns. The guns should certainly be in an absolutely top-class mechanical condition.

Old cartridge pressures were given in tons per square inch but, even if you know the conver-sions, do not attempt to translate tons into bars. The old 'tons' pressures were taken by a rather crude method which failed to detect sharp peaks of pressure, while the modern, computer-con-trolled equipment which measures in bars is much more accurate.

In general, you will enjoy your shooting much more if you choose cartridges with the minimum power to do the job in hand efficiently. There is nothing macho in shooting over-powerful car-tridges – they just wear out your gun more quickly and make your shoulder hurt!

12 THE MARKET PLACE

Here is a more detailed look at the guns you may find, some still new but mostly second-hand, on the British market.

ARAMBERRI

Back in the 1970s, if you were an aspiring clay shooter, you may have considered buying the Spanish-built Aramberri. It was highly affordable, yet it balanced and shot quite well and had a number of features usually found only on much more expensive offerings. In short, it was a poor man's Perazzi and the design similarity with the prestige Italian competition gun is quite striking.

No one in the gun trade can recall seeing a new Aramberri since the early 1980s, so any examples you find nowadays may well be beyond their 'best by' date, yet the gun was quite rugged and so a good one may still be a fair buy. The snag is that factory spares can no longer be found, but, considering the design similarities, many Perazzi and Kemen spares may fit.

Best buys
Given the fact that the gun is no longer available on the British market, consider only late-model guns in exceptional condition.

AYA

When affordable English guns started to disappear from the scene Anglo-Spanish Imports (ASI) of Snape, Suffolk, went to Spain for replacements and thus forged an enduring link with Aguirre y Aranzabal – the maker commonly known as AYA.

There is a huge variety of guns on both the new and the second-hand market. Side-by-sides in both boxlock and sidelock configurations predominate and all are strong, well-balanced, nononsense guns with a reputation for long life. Spares are generally cheap and are easily fitted.

The same may be said for the O/Us which, although less common, generally offer good value for money. A classic was the Coral, in both the boxlock and the sidelock configuration, and it shared many design features with the German-built Merkel. In fact, some of the spares are interchangeable. More common and cheaper is the Yeoman (not to be confused with their side-by-side gun of the same name), which comes in fixed and multichoke versions. None of the guns has any particular weaknesses.

Best buys
There isn't a bad one. The No.4 is as tough and simple a boxlock side-by-side as you will find and it handles well. Most O/Us are well-made and strong, but in no way exceptional. The old Coral, now available only on special order in sidelock or boxlock configuration, has real style, but buy carefully.

BAIKAL

The Russian-built Baikal is one of the workhorses of British shooting. It is cheap and cheerful as well as being efficient and long-lived. Unkind critics say that they are built from melted-down Soviet tanks, with wood from surplus sleepers from the Trans-Siberian Railway. This is not true; although the steel is quite basic it is very strong. The original factory woodwork is often rather short in the stock for British tastes and most stockers say it cannot be bent. For these reasons, guns fitted by the importer with a better grade of woodwork from Italy are worth seeking out.

There are side-by-sides and O/Us, all general-purpose fixed-chokes, some with double triggers and some with single. Most single-triggers have a cunningly hidden barrel selector: you push the trigger forward until it clicks to select the top barrel first.

The main enemy of the Baikal is dirt, which may make triggers and ejection sluggish. There are no particular mechanical drawbacks, although some older guns have rather greyish blacking.

Best buys
All the guns are strong and long-lived, although the machining on some models may be somewhat rough. Favourites are late-model, single-trigger Model 27Es with the Italian woodwork.

BENELLI

Italian-built Benelli semi-autos cycle on an unusual inertia system which, although reliant on recoil, is not a pure recoil-fed system. The quality is generally high, with misuse and general decrepitude being the only points to watch for when buying second-hand. The bolt, as on some Winchester models, has a turning head which locks it positively to the barrel at the moment of firing, rather like the famous Kalashnikov assault rifle. Some of the guns – particularly those in 20-gauge – are very light in weight; so, although the mechanism soaks up recoil well, make sure the weight suits you before buying. The mechanism has a generally very good ammunition tolerance, which is the plague of some semi-autos. As with all autos, check that the gun is a three-shot if you want to hold it on an ordinary shotgun certificate.

Best buys
The Super-90 models and the Montefeltro 20-bore are as good a selection of autos as you will find. If you want something really unusual look for a Centro with interchangeable, carbon-fibre ribs.

BERETTA

Beretta is Italy's biggest gunmaker, with a huge variety of models. They fall into four broad categories: boxlock O/Us based on the 600-series action, the ASE series (competition guns with drop-out trigger/tumbler mechanisms), the sidelock SO series of O/Us, and the semi-autos.

The 600 series includes the 686 and the 687, both models in competition and field-shooting configurations, and the 682, which is a pure competition gun in skeet, trap and sporting versions. None has any vices; but later models of the 682 for all disciplines have better balance and handling than the early guns, which tend to be a little sluggish. Early competition guns of all types were originally built to cycle on the old 32g competition load and, although most have been modified, if you do find a gun that will not pick up on the second barrel with a 28g shell, the chances are that it needs a lighter inertia block spring – which is cheap and easy for a gunsmith to fit.

The ASE series has never been imported in big numbers, but is available in trap, skeet and sporting rigs. It is a quality gun, with a price to match.

The SO sidelocks cost even more, and are available in sporting, trap, skeet and game versions. When buying one look at the wood in the area of the hand and the head – rough treatment has caused a few to crack in this area.

Among the autos you will find the discontinued A300, A301, A302 and A303 models in all configurations, with late model A303s being generally the best buys. The A304 was a stopgap gun between the 303 and the 390 series, and was never imported in large numbers. The current model (1998) is the AL390, which is an expensive but very efficient and pleasantly handling auto.

Note that all recent Berettas except trap and skeet versions have 3in (76mm) chambers and magnum proof, which, of course, does not prevent you from using any shorter cartridge through them. All the break-action Beretta O/Us hinge on replaceable stub pins. The letters EL after the gun's name indicate a higher quality and EELL models are the highest quality of all.

Best buys
With an excellent build quality and a well-informed importer, it is hard to go wrong. Some of the early 682 sporters were rather heavy and sluggish, and the 686 Essential is a bit light for long strings of shots on the clay ground. But that still leaves a big field.

BETTINSOLI

The Bettinsoli is a typical 'Italian design school' O/U in the budget price bracket: a shallow action, single trigger with the barrels hinged on stub pins. Of the more recent guns, the cheaper ones were called 'Classics', while the Silver Classics comprised a slightly more expensive range. Most versions were available in both 12- and 20-gauge, and among the Silver Classics were lightweight game guns with aluminium alloy actions. All recent guns are multichokes and a feature of them is the optional 'Plus Two' choke system, which provides extra-long choke tubes which protrude 2in from the muzzle, and this has the effect of lengthening the barrel. Thus a 28in gun may also be shot as a 30, and a 30in gun as a 32. No model had any particular mechanical problems and condition is the only real guide for buyers.

Best buys
The Silver Classic does not cost much more than the Classic and is better finished. The 20-bore Silver Classic is particularly nice if you are looking for the smaller gauge.

BROWNING

The break-action Brownings come in three main classifications: the B25 variants which are made in Belgium; the B125, which is assembled in Belgium from parts made in the Far East; and the B325/B425 family, all of which originate from Miroku in Japan. Classified with this last family is the Gti Ultra, more recently known as just the 'Ultra', which is also built by Miroku.

The modern B25 is essentially the same as that for which John Moses Browning filed patents in 1923, the main difference with most guns being that they have the mechanical single-trigger mechanism developed by John's son Val in the late 1930s. It is either blessed or cursed, depending on your point of view, with a non-detachable fore-end which slides forward for barrel release. John Moses said that he made the gun this way because, if he had to take one apart somewhere in the field where there was nowhere clean or convenient to place the pieces, he wanted to be able to hold the two main parts, one in each hand. The only other recent Browning to have this feature is the B125; all others have fully detachable fore-ends.

The sometimes confusing sequence of letter and numbers which follows the designation B25, such as B2G, C2G or D5G, refers to the standard of finish and the engraving. Of the many styles available, seventeen are illustrated in recent catalogues and there are many more 'standard' patterns as well as custom jobs engraved for individual clients. All are signed by the engravers.

A point to watch here is that, to be an authentic Browning model, engraving and other custom work must have been done in the Browning workshops at Herstal. There are also some very fine Browning B25s about which have been customized elsewhere, and some look like high-grade Browning patterns. There is nothing wrong with that provided that they are sold as what they are and not as official Browning versions. So, if you are offered what appears to be a high-grade Browning and there is any doubt about it, a call to Browning, quoting the serial number, will either put your mind at rest or sound a warning.

The B25 comes in a large variety of configurations for game shooting as well as all the main clay disciplines, and the B125 is available for game, sporting and trap in six different grades, including the black and gold Sporting F1 and Trap F1 finishes.

The Miroku-built B325 was renamed the B425 in 1975, the main difference between the two models being the method of barrel construction. Miroku barrels had always been made on 'chopper-lump' principles, in which the lump was forged integrally with the lower tube, but the change was made to the more economic and possibly stronger monobloc method in 1975.

The back-bored, long-choked Browning Gti Ultra competition gun (in skeet, sporting and trap versions) was similarly affected, and became known simply as the Ultra. For those who do not like the stark black actions of this family, the guns to look for are the Gti S and the Ultra S, which employ the same barrel technology with silver polished, engraved actions. Comparatively rare in this country are the Anson (boxlock) and the BSL (sidelock) side-by-sides. This latter gun is the only Browning sidelock shotgun, all the rest are boxlocks.

The original Browning semi-auto was the Auto 5, first made in 1905. International sales have now topped six million. The gun is extremely reliable, but it works on the old, long-recoil principle and is best with cartridges of 32g or heavier. The modern Browning auto is the gas-fed Gold, late models of which have the wide-bore, long-choke technology of the Ultra O/U series. In between these two there have been other short-recoil and gas-operated models.

Brownings have no specific mechanical faults, but all are made of a very strong but relatively plain steel which does rust if it is not looked after and cleaned properly. The B125 seems to be particularly at risk, and barrels and chambers should be checked especially carefully when buying second-hand.

Best buys

Where do we start? Most Brownings handle well, although the Citori – the predecessor of the B325 – was made to an American market formula and was something of a heavy handful. My personal favourites on the second-hand market are the B325 and the Gti or the Ultra S model.

CLASSIC DOUBLES

The Classic Doubles firm came to the United Kingdom in the late 1980s, when Winchester withdrew from the break-action shotgun market, taking with them their relatively newly introduced 5000, 6500 and 8500 series. These Japanese-built guns were the swan song of Winchester's famous 101 series – of which more later – and Classic Doubles sold late-production guns under their own name. They were Winchesters in everything but label; the reader is therefore referred to the section below on the relevant Winchester models for details.

For their next gun Classic Doubles went to Marocchi of Italy. It was the M90, which was a totally different design concept from the Winchester. It was a low-level gun, pivoting on stub pins, with rather Beretta-like handling. In 1992 it was superseded by the improved M92. It is also the only gun on the British market to be offered in a specific version for women: the M92 Ladysport. The rainbow colours on the sides of the action may be nothing more than styling for the American market, but the weight and stock dimensions do genuinely suit most women shooters. The weight is not so low as to cause recoil problems, balance is good, and the rather full stock fits better to the average woman's slimmer jaw line. Cheaper versions of the 'male' M92 are sold under the American Sportsman label.

Best buys

Some of the old Winchester-based models are superb, but there is a spares problem. The M92 is definitely the best of the rest.

FABARM

The best-known of the Italian-built Fabarms on the British market is the single-trigger, O/U multichoke Gamma, although there are similarly constructed, fixed-choke models going back fifteen years or more. All are sturdy and strong, although it may be rather irksome to get the firing pins out of some models.

In recent years the Fabarm semi-automatics have become much more popular, particularly with the introduction of the competitively-priced Euro 3. It weighs $6^1/_2$lb, which is a good weight for a pigeon or rough-shooting gun, and the example I tested had a very good ammunition tolerance, all the way from heavy 'fowling loads to some quite light 28g offerings.

Barrels on all Fabarms seem particularly sturdy, and all late-model guns are internally chromed. As with all well-used multichokes, look out for stuck or otherwise abused chokes on very old guns which may not have had much care.

Best buys
The Gamma has been around a long time and has not been found wanting. It is one of the better medium-priced O/Us on the second-hand market.

FIAS

Never heard of it? FIAS models were never imported in large numbers, but that did not stop Browning from going to this Italian factory for their lowest-priced gun, the Medallist. All comments about the Medallist apply equally to the FIAS, so read on ...

Best buys
Either the FIAS is no longer imported or the importer hides a dim light under a very large bushel! Buy a Medallist, with all the Browning backing.

FRANCHI

This prestige Italian maker has produced some excellent guns over the years – mostly break-actions designed for the competition disciplines. There have also been some excellent gas-fed semi-autos. In recent years, however, there has been a spares problem and, at the time of writing, the future availability of Franchi spares is unknown. Make inquiries on this point at the time of buying and, if spares are available, there is every chance that you will get an excellent gun.

GAMBA

Which Gamba? All are high-quality guns, but not all come from the same factory. The latest, from Renato Gamba, is called the Daytona and is a very-high class competition gun designed primarily for the American market. However, small numbers are available over here and the quality and the workmanship are beyond fault. Older Gambas, such as the Gold, were made in another factory by one of Renato's relatives and, although well made (with Perazzi-style, dropout trigger mechanisms), they were not in quite the same league.

Best buys
It depends on how much you want to spend. You will get a well-conditioned Gold for about £800 (1998 value), but a Daytona, even on the second-hand market, is going to be in the region of £3,000 for some years to come.

INVESTARM

Cheap and cheerful is the phrase for this simple, Italian-made O/U. It comes in folding and non-folding versions, in 12-bore, 20-bore and 0.410in. The mechanism is about as basic as you can get and, at the price, the guns are hard to fault.

Best buys

The slightly more expensive non-folding model is best. If the folding model becomes rather free-working in the hinge, you will find that when you open it to reload the end of the barrel swings down and may crack you on the kneecap or the shin. Yet who but a poacher needs a folding gun?

KEMEN

This gun caused quite a stir when it arrived on the British scene in 1993. It looked like a Perazzi and it shot like one, but it was not as expensive. It had the same steady handling and the same drop-out trigger. It is also very well made – in Spain – and a go-ahead importer persuaded the leading clay shooters George Digweed and Richard Faulds to take up with the marque. Thus assured of publicity, the Kemen went from strength to strength. There are models for all the main clay disciplines and field shooting.

Best buys

With such a recent importing history it is hard to go wrong, but do not expect to find a flood of guns on the second-hand market.

KRIEGHOFF

This is one of Germany's prestige guns, built with the efficiency and precision you would expect. Most of the competition guns are boxlocks, built around the design of the late, lamented Remington 3200 break action. A feature of this design is that there is no conventional locking bolt, but the top of the action slides backwards on a dovetail and closes over the top tube of the barrel set. This creates a sighting plane that takes some getting used to, but other than that the gun is hard to fault. Also available in very small numbers in the United Kingdom is the Ulm sidelock, which I had never seen until I tested one in late 1997. It had, however, been around in Europe and the USA since

1958. The Ulm works on a different principle, with an under bolt and a cross bolt, and matches the top-grade Beretta SOs and Perazzis for quality.

Best buys

If you want a Krieghoff, you are already a specialist and know exactly what you want. Just look out for general wear and tear.

LANBER

The design of the Spanish-built Lanber O/U goes back more than twenty years. Early importers called it the Eibargun and the Animo Express; the name Lanber was established when Gunmark took over in 1977. In the next two decades they were to sell 20,000 to British shooters.

It has always been a good, strong, long-lasting gun and its failings can be lived with. In fact, most Lanber owners never have a single thing go wrong. However, pre-1982 guns differ slightly from later models and may be a little more expensive to repair. The failings amount to few: a slightly fragile safety catch spring on some guns, and a small screw near the root of the trigger which may shoot loose in others. Both faults are easily remedied.

The 30in magnum model came out in 1978 and the first Sporting Multichoke in 1983. The few De Luxe Skeet and Trap models still around date back to 1984–85. The Barry Simpson-designed Sporter came out in 1987, and Sporters with schnabel fore-ends and the 30in barrel option appeared in 1989. A comparatively recent newcomer is the Lanber Victoria semi-auto.

Best buys

The post-1987 O/U sporters – the ones which came out after the clay-shooting champion Barry Simpson had redesigned the woodwork – are the most popular and most comfortable to shoot, too. On guns which have obviously had a hard life look out for stuck choke tubes.

LAURONA

Some people think that the Spanish-built Laurona looks a big, awkward handful. In fact, most models balance, point and shoot far better than they look, and the Derby game model is a very good gun with nice handling. All models are particularly suitable for hard environments in that the barrels are blacked with the application of black chromium plate and are thus extremely resistant to corrosion, including that encountered on salt marshes. All modern Laurona O/Us are multichokes and field versions usually have 3in magnum chambers.

Best buys
If you wish to shoot long strings of magnums watch the weight because some field versions are a little on the light side for shells of this power. Otherwise all models are mechanically sound in design and materials. Late-model guns have fluted fore ends with straight-cut ridges rather than chequering.

LINCOLN

Lincoln is the name given to a series of Italian-built O/Us by the importers Nickersons. All fall into the value-for-money range and many are good general-purpose guns. There is also a big-bore 'fowling gun: the 10-bore in the Lincoln range is the 32in Premier, which is available in single- and double-trigger versions. It has $3^{1}/_{2}$in magnum chambers, chromed bores and is choked $^{3}/_{4}$ and full. The weight is 10 to 11lb.

Best buys
There is nothing special to look for: all guns are mechanically sound and the Premier is one of the few 10-bore O/Us available in the United Kingdom.

MEDALLIST

When Browning's British operation wanted a cheap but serviceable gun they went to Italy because neither they nor their partners Miroku were geared up to build to the specification required. Its name was to be the Medallist and the first gun, which was imported for only a year, was a disaster. Almost every one sold finished up back in the workshop with some fault or other and the order was hastily cancelled. It was replaced by a gun built by FIAS, which turned out to be a winner.

Up to 1991 there was a fixed-choke trap gun, and since then the Medallist has been available only in its multichoke configuration. As such, it is an excellent sporter/general purpose gun, and there is a pretty little 20-bore in the range. All versions have gained an excellent reputation for reliability.

Best buys
If you can find a second-hand trap version, as I did for a gun test in 1996, you will find it is one of the cheapest specialist trap guns around. It is also a good buy because all the sporter spares fit: only the barrels and woodwork were different. All other guns should be bought on condition and – fortunately – I have not seen one of those early guns on the second-hand racks for years.

MERKEL

The Merkel factory is at Suhl, in the former East Germany. This means that before German reunification the guns enjoyed artificially low prices in the West, because factory wages were low and East Germany was crying out for hard currency. But there was never anything cheap or nasty about a Merkel: both the boxlock and the sidelock O/Us were made to high quality and the same basic design as the AYA Coral.

There is something different and attractive about a Merkel. It is not just another coil-spring-powered boxlock O/U, and neither is it a Browning or a Beretta look-alike. It locks with both an under-bolt and a high-mounted cross-bolt which engages with lugs which form extensions of the breech end of the top barrel, and it is powered by V-springs. It has totally different lines from the average O/U, and most examples make fine game guns. The sidelock versions are particularly well made, and the 303E is one of the finest guns of its type I have ever tested, with workmanship quite the equal of a 'best' London gun.

The boxlocks are the most familiar on the British market and, although they are not that common, they are worth seeking out if you want something different.

Best buys
Gouges and wear on the upper barrel extensions where they engage with the cross-bolt indicate a gun that is past its best. The ejectors are retained by two tiny screws in the bottom of the barrel extensions, and if these snap off they are awkward to replace. Other than that, buy both single- and double-trigger models on general condition. Do not remove the action floorplate unless you know what you are doing: springs will fly out and they are very difficult to replace.

MIROKU

Miroku is Japan's most prolific gunmaker and, as previously mentioned, makes all break-action Brownings except the prestige B25 derivatives. Its own guns share many design similarities with the Brownings and for a long time now the company has paid particular attention to handling qualities and stock dimensions.

Late models include the MK60 (fixed choke), the MK70 and the MK38 in sporter and trap configurations. All are available in several grades and the MK38 Trap is one of the finest trap guns available at its price. Previous models were designated 6000, 7000 and 3800, and the guns with shorter numbers came before them.

All Mirokus have proved rugged and reliable as well as sweetly handling. Most guns after firing many thousands of cartridges suffer from firing pins with cratered tips, but this fault is easily and cheaply rectified.

Best buys
The only models to avoid are some of the very early guns which were powered by V-springs rather than coil springs, but that is only because many will now be past their best. When buying a Miroku of any age, look at the tip of the bottom barrel firing pin and, if it has a pin-hole crater in the end, get it changed. Otherwise all guns in good condition are good value for money.

NIKKO

The Japanese-built Nikko is no longer in production, and that is a pity because it was well built and had particularly good handling qualities. The most familiar model was the 5000, in field, trap and skeet specifications.

Best buys
The last guns came in during the early 1980s, so all are going to be rather long in the tooth by now. Added to that is a spares problem, so consider only guns in immaculate condition. A common fault is that, with long use, ejectors become splayed outwards and eventually override cartridge heads. They can be bent back with care, but let a gunsmith do it: as we have remarked before, the responsibility will be his if he breaks it.

PERAZZI

The Italian-built Perazzi is, debatably, the world's most famous trap gun. A fact often forgotten is that the company's skeet, sporting and game guns are equally finely constructed, but it is the trap models which have the reputation in international and top-end domestic competition.

Late models include game trap and sporter versions of the MX8, with or without the famous Perazzi drop-out trigger group; the MX10 trap with its adjustable stock and rib; and the MX1B. All guns are available built to the owner's specification, with some beautiful engraving options and a choice of gauges with most models.

Best buys
All guns in good condition are good second-hand investments, if the price is right.

REMINGTON

Remington of Ilion, New York, is among the world's leading firearms manufacturers, and its most famous shotgun ever was the gas-fed Model 1100 semi-auto. It was made continually from 1963 to 1987, and it rapidly became the standard by which all other semi-autos were judged. It was available in many grades in skeet, trap and field specifications, but there never was a sporter for the simple reason that the Americans did not know the discipline until the end of the 1980s. That did not stop many British sporting shooters enjoying success with field models.

In 1987 this model was replaced by the 11-87 in 12-gauge, and the 20-gauge 1100 carried on. But such was the demand for the old gun in 12-gauge that it has since reappeared in limited production runs.

From the original twenty-four-year production run there are far too many different models to list and there are also a number of 'hybrids' about because barrels, actions and woodwork are totally interchangeable. In standard form there were at least fifteen different variations in 12-bore, plus 16-bores, 20-bores, 28-bores and 0.410in, in different specifications for skeet, trap, field shooting and wildfowling. There was also an American-market Deer Gun, with rifle sights and designed to shoot solid slugs. True left-handed versions, with the ejection port on the left and a reversed safety button, came out in 1972.

Guns imported from the mid-1960s until 1970 have German proof marks and an additional three- or four-digit number, different from the serial number, stamped on the left side of the receiver, towards the front. All the rest have English marks.

The current Remington semi-auto is the 11-87 Premier, late models of which are available only with the much-improved lightweight barrel. The Sporter, restricted to three shots but based on a four-shot version rather than the familiar five-shot, balances and handles particularly well.

Remington also made the break-action 3200 in various guises from 1973 until 1984. In design it is similar to the modern Krieghoff boxlock.

Best buys
Model 1100s, unless from one of the post-1987 batches, need to be examined particularly carefully for worn-out internal rails, fatigue cracks in the receiver body (particularly just behind the bolt handle slot), and general signs of age. Extractor claws and spring links behind the bolt are frequently required but easily fitted spares. Early examples of the Model 11-87 were somewhat clumsy, and later models with the lightweight barrel are much preferred. All 3200s are going to be a little old now, so check their condition carefully. The break-action Model 32 was made before World War II.

RIZZINI

The most common gun in the United Kingdom is the E. Rizzini, which is a cheap and cheerful general-purpose gun and usually excellent value for money. It may shoot loose and, if the sears get worn, when you open them to load you may get the impression of pushing the barrel down against a spring for the last part of its movement. However, the importers – Sportsmarketing, of Colchester, Essex – will put all problems right at a very reasonable cost.

Best buys
None is better than another – just buy on general condition.

RUGER

The most familiar Ruger shotgun in the United Kingdom is the Red Label, with its all-stainless action and generally very tough construction. There are field and sporting clays models in 12- and 20-gauge, and one model with a straight-hand stock. All late 12- and 20-bore models have 3in chambers and the 12s have back-bored (0.743in) barrels. Barrels are particularly strong, and are built to accept US factory steel loads.

Best buys
Check the handling because some models are rather slow and heavy feeling by European standards. However, weight and steadiness may be an advantage if you want to fire primarily big magnum loads.

SHADOW

This Japanese manufacturer made some lovely competition guns with extremely smooth handling. However, all will be getting old now and, at the time of writing, the few available spares are on the shelves of the original importers, Gunmark.

Best buys
Buy only guns in excellent condition and do be prepared to have parts made if anything breaks.

WINCHESTER

Winchester are – it is to hoped only temporarily – out of the break-action shotgun business. Their most famous O/U model, the Winchester 101, was designed by Winchester engineers in the USA but made in Japan by Olin Kodensha. The Olin Corporation, Winchester's parent company in the era, at one time had a 50 per cent holding in the Kodensha plant.

The original 101 was introduced, in 12-bore, in 1963. The smaller gauges of 20, 28 and 0.410 followed three years later, although they were relatively uncommon in Europe right until the end of the production run. Also introduced in 1966 were magnum field models, a skeet gun and a trap gun. The XTR model, which replaced previous field models, came out in 1981, together with a 3in chambered waterfowl version. Diamond-grade guns, in trap and skeet configurations, became available in 1982. A British favourite, the 101 Super Grade game gun, appeared in the early 1980s. Multichoke versions of all guns date back to the late 1970s, the first models having tubes with externally knurled rings.

Later European market derivatives – the 5000, the 6500 and the 8500 - came at the end of the production run in the late 1980s and were among the best-handling of a generally well-behaved breed.

The design of the 101 was a simple development of well-established Browning principles, with all the mechanical components stacked neatly one on top of another in a relatively deep action. The gun hinges on a full-width cross-pin and is locked by a full-width bolt running along the action floor.

The Winchester side-by-side of the era was the Model 23 which, with its high rib and pistol-grip stock, was one of the few side-by-sides ever to have much of a following among clay shooters. In addition to the standard models, there were lightweights and heavy duck versions, a 20-bore and a multichoke 12. Most of the guns imported into the United Kingdom had 3in chambers. The model disappeared at the same time as the O/U.

Semi-autos included the short-lived 1400 and the long-running 1400 Mk2, both gas-fed. The 1400 in both forms was a medium-priced, no-nonsense gun but, unlike the 101, it never became a classic. It was constantly under the shadow of the much better, although admittedly more expensive, Remington models.

Best buys

There is a spares problem with all 101 derivatives, but the gun now has such a cult following that enthusiasts are winkling them out, worldwide, and some new parts are being made by third parties. The 101 also suffers from the same firing pin problems as Miroku models, and ejector kickers are starting to break on some of the older guns. Ejector rods are rather spindly and tend to bend and stick. For the best-handling competition guns, go for the late-model 6500s. Buy all 101s and derivatives and model 23s with care, bearing in mind that prices now seem to be rising rather than falling and that spares may never be easy to find. Just look for general wear and tear in semi-auto 1400s. The break-action Winchester 1001 was withdrawn from the market on safety grounds and, to the best of my knowledge, all of them sold in the United Kingdom were rounded up.

13 SHOTGUN CLEANING

In the old days of black gunpowder, gun cleaning was a vitally important task which had to be carried out rigorously as soon as possible after a gun had been used. Both powders and primers left highly corrosive residues and the barrel of an uncleaned gun soon became internally rusted, and eventually pitted and greatly weakened. Barrels had to be meticulously cleaned, and the old-time shooter did not have the modern range of cleaning compounds to help him. Barrels were often cleaned by pouring boiling water through them and the whole process was quite tedious.

Modern propellant powders are not nearly so corrosive and corrosive primers are also now a rarity. Some guns have internally chromed barrels and modern cleaning solvents are very effective. On the down side, there may be a slight problem with acid residues from plastic cartridge components, and multichoke tubes may stick in if they are not thoroughly cleaned after shooting. So it is still wise to clean all shotguns as soon as possible after shooting, but efficient cleaning is not nearly the chore that it once was.

At this point you may ask why gun barrels are not made of stainless steel. In fact, nickel-chrome stainless steel was first developed as part of the search for a non-corroding barrel steel, but it proved unsuitable for shotguns because it has such poor heat conductivity. It may also be difficult and expensive to machine, and that is why barrels continue to be made of relatively plain alloy steels which may rust if they are neglected.

This selection of cleaning rod accessories includes bronze brushes and plastic jags, both of which are requirements for efficient gun cleaning.

EQUIPMENT AND MATERIALS

The equipment for cleaning is quite simple and inexpensive. You will need a cleaning rod long enough to pass right through the bore, a phosphor-bronze brush and a soft metal or plastic jag. You will also need a supply of clean rags, and a few cotton buds for getting into nooks and crannies could be handy. Do not waste your

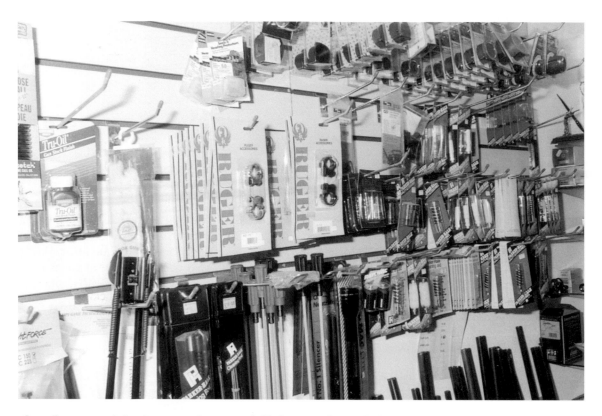

Gun oil, grease and cleaning accessories are available from gun shop racks in convenient blister packs.

money on precut cleaning patches or fabric patches which can be torn off a roll: kitchen paper or toilet paper is just as effective, far cheaper and present in every household.

You will also need some cleaning solvent and there are several different types. The stuff I prefer can be bought in spray cans or bottles, and familiar brand names are Napier, Warthog and Browning Legia Spray. With a modern gun you can also use WD40, but this preparation should not be used on old English guns because, in the long term, it may remove the blacking. Most modern chemical blacking processes are resistant to it.

Then there is another type which smells strongly of nitrobenzene – like old-fashioned boot polish. Familiar brand names of this are Hoppes No.9 and Parker Hale 09. Both are great preparations for getting metallic fouling

out of rifle barrels, but they are stronger than you need for most shotgun cleaning and they also smell most unpleasantly. They can be useful for getting heavy fouling out of the gas ports and cylinders of semi-automatic shotguns; but you should also remember that they are designed to dissolve brass and other copper-based alloys such as bronze, so if you use the material with a phosphor-bronze brush, then wash the brush in paraffin or white spirit afterwards because a brush that is left wet with the stuff may actually decrease in size.

You will also need some gun oil, and there are many brands on gun shop shelves, all equally good. Gun oil is relatively thin; but if, like me, you fill up your general household oil can with the dregs from car oil cans do not use this on your gun. It is far too thick and will gum up the works if it gets into the action. It has also been suggested that some of the additives in car lubricating oils are not to kind too guns in the long term. If you find yourself without gun oil use a thin household oil such as '3-in-1' or a light cycle oil.

Finally, you will need a small pot or tube of grease. You can buy gun grease, but otherwise use the grade recommended for packing car wheel bearings. Do not use Vaseline, it has very poor lubricating properties, although it is a good rust inhibitor for long-term storage.

As for working area, a shed or garage – preferably with a few square feet of bench space – is ideal. If you work in the kitchen or a utility room, remember that bronze brushes, when they emerge from muzzles, may spray filthy black muck all over the place, so a few sheets of newspaper on the floor, table or worktop may prevent domestic disharmony.

A Cleaning Programme

I have a cleaning regime that I always follow and in that way I do not forget parts of it. Here it is:
• Take off the fore-end and remove the barrels. Put the stock/action and the fore-end aside.
• If the gun is a multichoke, take the choke tubes out. I know that some authorities prefer to clean the choke tubes while they are in the gun on the grounds that otherwise cleaning debris may get into the threads. But if you do the job properly this does not happen.
• Squirt enough cleaning solvent down the barrels just to cover the walls right through and leave it to work for a few minutes.
• Put the phosphor-bronze brush on the cleaning rod and pass it right through each barrel from chamber to muzzle, allowing it to come out of the end before you pull it back. As you go through the forcing cones (the tapered parts immediately in front of the chambers) and the threaded areas of a multichoke, you can twist the brush clockwise as you go through. This adds to the scrubbing motion and cleans the threads quite efficiently.
• Take off the bronze brush and put the jag on. Wrap around it sufficient paper to make it a push fit through the barrels. Half a sheet of

kitchen paper, folded twice, is usually about right. Pass a fresh piece of paper through each barrel, taking it off the jag when it emerges from the muzzle. Do not pull it back through or you will be putting the dirt back in again.
• Look through both barrel tubes. They should be bright and shiny all the way through. If there are any marks, put in more solvent, wait a few minutes and go back to the bronze brush stage. If you get a slimy or stringy deposit on the brush it is plastic fouling from cartridge wads and you must get it all out.
• If the gun is a multichoke, use the thread-cleaning attachment on the choke key, if there is one. If not, examine the threads carefully and clean them with paper if they are still dirty. The best way is to pass the paper in, on the jag, from the chamber end and turn it clockwise as it goes through the threaded area.
• The barrels should now be totally clean inside. Wipe the outside of them over with a lightly oiled cloth and expect some light soot in the muzzle area. A lightly oiled cotton bud may be used to remove dirt from awkward corners under ribs.
• Examine the ejectors. They should slide freely in their tracks, with no gritty feeling. If there is grit in the ejector tracks you will have to take them out for cleaning. In any case, wipe any old, dirty oil from the ejector areas and replace it with fresh, using only a few drops. The area should be just damp with oil, not swimming in it. Any dirt under the ejectors may be removed with an oily cotton bud.
• Clean the choke tubes, if there are any, with solvent – not forgetting any additional tubes you have used during the day. You can use the bronze brush on the insides, followed with paper, while an old toothbrush will usually get any obstinate dirt out of the threads. Lightly grease the threads and replace the tubes.
• Work on the barrels is now complete, although, if they are not internally chromed, you may wish to pass through a final piece of paper with a very little oil on it. Do not use too much or it may run back through the firing pin holes into the action when the gun is stored and

eventually damage the woodwork.

• Examine the fore-end and wipe any dirt off the metal parts with a lightly oiled cloth. Make particularly sure that there is no grit in the knuckle area of the iron. If there is any ejector mechanism within the fore-end it should be clean and very lightly oiled – just a tiny drop on the bearing surfaces.

• Examine the action, wiping the outside with a lightly oiled cloth. Use the cloth or cotton buds to get any dirt out of the inside. Any stuff that looks like tiny grains of dark sawdust will be grains of unburnt powder. Any visible mechanism should also be lightly oiled – just slightly damp with it. Old grease should be wiped off the knuckles.

• You are now ready to reassemble the gun. Before you do so, put a tiny smear of grease on the knuckles and the hinge pin or stub pins.

And that's it. When you have done it a few times it may take no longer than it has taken to read these instructions. You will do more harm than good if you oil the stock every time you use the gun; you should just rub off any mud with a soft cloth and, if the shine has gone dull, restore it with a smear of wax furniture polish, not the stuff from a spray can which often contains solvents which can do oil finishes no good. You can get mud out of chequering with either an old toothbrush or a nailbrush. Never use a wire brush.

IF THE GUN IS WET

If your gun has become very wet there is a further precaution you may take. First of all, wipe it as dry as you can when you get back to your car and before you put it in its slip. If the slip itself is damp leave the gun in it only as long as you need to because nothing turns a gun rusty faster than its being allowed to warm up in a damp slip. After a game shoot any traces of bird blood should be wiped off immediately; blood promotes very rapid rusting and unattended drops leave little 'fleck' marks in the blacking.

When you get home again dry the gun as well as you can, and then follow the normal cleaning routine. If the woodwork is wet, do not try to dry it in front of any heat source or it may warp and crack. Just rub it dry and let any further drying take place naturally and at room temperature.

If you think water has got into the action take the stock off, if you know how. The metal of the action itself, minus the wood, may be dried on an ordinary, water-filled radiator but, again, the wood should be allowed to dry naturally. If you cannot take the stock off, take it to a gunsmith for professional cleaning as soon as possible.

There is no need to clean the internal parts of a gun's action very often; about once a year for a gun that enjoys average use is quite sufficient, and even then there is no need to take it to

A nail brush like this will get mud and dirt out of chequering without doing damage. Greasy dirt often responds to a lick of white spirit before brushing.

pieces. My usual procedure is just to remove the stock and wash out the mechanism with copious squirts of WD40. The mechanism is then left to drip and dry on newspaper and, when it is completely dry, a very sparing amount of gun oil is put on all bearing surfaces. Literally one tiny drop, applied with a cocktail stick or the little, pointed dropper that comes built into the stopper of some gun oil cans, on each bearing surface is quite enough. Even with this tiny amount of oil any apparent excess should be dabbed off with clean cloth or absorbent paper.

If you do not feel competent to take the stock off, your gunsmith will include internal cleaning in an annual service.

SEMI-AUTOS

Semi-auto barrels are cleaned in exactly the same way as those on break-action guns, with two additional steps. You should carefully clean any indentation in the rearward barrel extension into which the bolt locking device fits, and any lugs or grooves used in other types of lock-up.

You should also clean out the gas ports and the inside of the gas cylinder. Pipe cleaners are handy for the ports and any hard carbon will usually yield to nitrobenzene-based solvents.

The gas piston and the forward end of the magazine tube also need careful cleaning. If you do this regularly really hard carbon will not have the chance to build up. I once had a particularly hard job with a badly neglected Beretta piston and mentioned it in the magazine. One reader recommended an old naval cure for dirty, corroded components: just boiling them in an old saucepan full of soapy water. I tried it on the Beretta piston and it worked brilliantly! You should also wipe all the visible parts of the magazine tube and the links between the piston and the bolt.

Every few months you need to drop the trigger mechanism out of a semi-auto. This is usually a simple operation involving the striking out of a couple of pins, when the whole trigger/cartridge carrier group should drop out in your hand. Again, a good dose of WD40 usually does the trick, followed by drying and relubrication. While you are doing this you can also

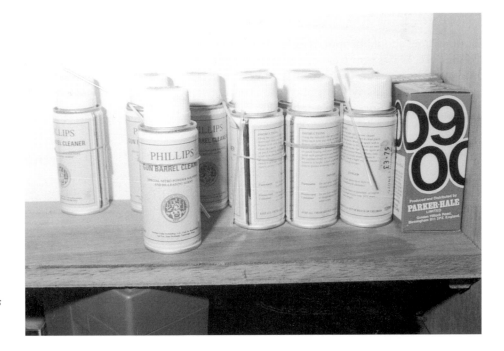

Most gun shops stock a good selection of bore-cleaning solvents. Both of these preparations will shift really obstinate dirt.

take out the bolt and clean it, and wipe out the inside of the receiver with a lightly oiled cloth. When doing this watch out for sharp edges on the rails.

Be particularly careful of the area around the piston of a semi-auto. More than a tiny smear of oil usually gets thrown back into your face, as black as soot, on the next occasion that you fire, and many guns work best if this area is left clean but bone dry.

MULTICHOKE TUBES

If ever a choke tube gets stuck in apply as much pressure as you can with the key and your fingers, but no more. If you extend the key with bits of metal tube and use them as levers you may do more harm than good. If the tube is still stuck, warm the barrels gently (no hotter than they will get on a water-filled domestic radiator) and soak the tube area in very thin oil or diesel oil. If that does not work, seek professional help.

GUN CABINETS

Your cabinet should be mounted in a dry part of your house. If it is prone to condensation or you live near the sea you will need to check your guns for rust regularly. You may also consider putting in some sort of rust-inhibiting device. There are felt pads which can be sprayed with a slowly evaporating rust inhibitor, porous bags of material which do much the same thing, or blocks of sponge which emit rust-inhibiting fumes. Also remember that some people have 'rusty fingers' – slightly acid perspiration which may leave rusty fingerprints. If you are one of these people wipe your gun with a clean cloth every time you handle it.

SAFETY IN THE HOME

I have read any number of inquest and incident

reports when, after an unintended shooting, the person who fired the shot said, 'It went off accidentally while I was cleaning it.' How could it have done? In order for a gun to be fired it has to be loaded, closed and the trigger has to be pulled. Those are three different, conscious, physical actions which cannot be performed 'accidentally'. In these terms there can be no such things as gun accidents – just gun incidents, all of which are somebody's direct fault. There can be no excuses.

Furthermore, there is no need, ever, to load a gun while it is being cleaned. If you want to check the firing mechanism, the ejection or the trigger pulls, then use snap caps. They are totally safe and will not damage your gun's mechanism.

A live cartridge (right), contrasted with a snap cap. Do not confuse the two!

A FEW GENERAL RULES

- Always be very sparing with lubricating oil.
- Don't let lubricating oil soak into woodwork.
- Dry wet guns as soon as possible, but not with heat.
- Thoroughly dry wet gun slips before using them again.
- If you are in a situation where you cannot clean a gun properly at least wipe the outside metal parts with a lightly oiled cloth and poke a bit of lightly oiled rag through each barrel with a stick.
- The sooner guns are cleaned after being shot, the easier the cleaning process is.
- Never leave bits of oily rag in barrels with the thought that you are saving your gun from rust. They do not do much good and you may forget them, with dire consequences.
- Even if you have meticulously cleaned your gun yourself, always check the barrels for obstructions before loading.

14 THE WOODWORK

HORROR STORIES

Gun woodwork gets damaged in some totally bizarre accidents. Guns fall out of cars, get run over (usually by their owners), dropped and trodden on. One stocker tells me that much of his work comes from guns which have been laid across the back seats of cars, both in and out of slips, and sat on by heavy people. It is all too easy when, after a shoot, you are trying to clamber into a car that is already full of wet dogs, shot game, dripping coats and muddy wellingtons because getting away from a wet shoot usually has some resemblance to Napoleon's retreat from Moscow.

My personal prize goes to the story I heard about a totally weird wildfowling accident. While the shooter was enjoying a hot coffee from his flask after a good morning's sport on the marshes, a heavy missile whistled past his ear, hit his gun with a sharp crack and took a chip out of his stock. At first he wondered who could have thrown a stone in such a lonely place, but close examination showed the damage to have been done by a shellfish which had been dropped from a great height by a passing sea bird. His insurers must have had a laugh over that one! I have had a stock chipped by a falling clay splinter, which made a far more plausible story and is, in fact, quite a common accident. The moral is to keep your gun slipped when it is not in use.

To abnormal accidents you may add the fact that some gunwoodwork is fragile in places. Stocks which are cross- or diagonally-grained in the hand are always suspect and should be avoided when buying, and the very nature of the O/U design means that fore-end wood has some vulnerable places, usually at the back where it joins the iron and also has to provide clearance for ejector kickers. Such areas may be thin and prone to cracking, particularly if there are sharp angles in the wood. Remember that cracks usually start in the sharp corners of all engineering materials and all structures become stronger if the corners have a relatively large radius.

GOOD INTENTIONS

Stocks and fore-ends can also be killed by misplaced kindness. Oiled wood may look superb after a fresh coat of linseed, but too many coats can soften it if it is at all porous, which is why most gunsmiths recommend a little hard wax polish rather than oil for day-to-day care. The application of oil is really only a once-a-year job, and then it should be applied only if the stock really needs it. The exception is if the gun gets very wet and the surface takes on a milky hue. In that case, after the stock has thoroughly dried at room temperature, apply just a couple of drops of oil with the palm of the hand and do not oil the chequering. Varnished stocks usually need no maintenance other than an occasional buffing with a small amount of wax polish. Use oil on top of varnish and it just goes sticky, picks up dust and eventually looks worse than it did before you started. Also remember that, as previously mentioned, if oil is left in the barrel of a gun after cleaning it may run back through the firing pin holes, over the mechanism of the action and eventually into the woodwork.

CRACKING

Most cracks in woodwork, if they are caught early enough, can be repaired. If you get at them as soon as you notice them, oil will not have chance to get in and ruin the adhesive qualities of glue. The best adhesive to use for repairs is an epoxy resin such as Araldite, and the variety which takes several hours or overnight to cure is better than the five-minute variety. The first seems to dry very hard, while the second seems to stay slightly rubbery.

If you can do so without making matters worse, lever the crack open with something like a bit of shim steel or an old feeler gauge or even a strip cut from the side of a tin can, then warm the epoxy to make it runny and drip it in. If you have to, use your levering tool to push it right into the crack, then clean off any excess on the outside, tape or clamp the crack firmly and leave the job overnight to cure. If a crack goes right through a section of wood make sure that you get enough adhesive into it to come out the other side, so that the repair is as strong as possible.

A bad crack may also be pinned, if the wood in the area is thick enough. You will need a very tiny drill – about 2mm – and a thin dowel of similar diameter carved from hard, straight-grained wood. Excellent pins which are both thin and strong may be cut from the walls of thick bamboo canes. Having prepared the pin, drill carefully down through the crack and fill up both the crack and the drill hole with epoxy. All that remains is for the pin to be inserted and any surplus of epoxy wiped off before the job is taped or clamped for curing. The area of a crack in the thin wall of a fore-end may be further reinforced by gluing a patch cut from thin nylon material to the inside, provided that the tiny extra thickness does not rub on the barrel or foul the action of ejector kickers.

When you consider the cost of a new stock, it is always worthwhile attempting a repair, or having a stocker trying to do one for you. Some surprisingly large cracks can be glued and pinned, despite the fact that many old gun books say that they cannot. Remember that in the old days the common woodworking glue was made from animal residues (boiled-up hooves and horns), while adhesives made of modern, synthetic materials are much stronger.

However, cracks can be repaired only provided that they are clean and free from oil. You can sometimes get oil out of a crack by washing it with alcohol and letting it thoroughly dry before the repair is attempted, although stocks that are heavily soaked in oil are often impossible to repair safely.

REFINISHING A STOCK

Every shooter, at least once in his lifetime, gets the urge to refinish a stock completely. Often the stock has been factory-finished with polyurethane varnish, which eventually picks up scratches and scars and looks unsightly. In any case, most shooters prefer the traditional English oil finish, or something which looks like it.

The first task is to get off the old varnish. You can scrape it with a knife or the back of a plane blade, but this is laborious and there is always a danger of removing slivers of wood from critical areas which must fit to the metal or from the chequering. The use of paint stripper avoids these problems, but it should be done with the woodwork removed from the gun. You should also remove any plastic parts, as I have discovered – to my cost – that paint stripper eats some plastics just as efficiently as it eats old varnish.

The dissolved varnish will usually come off with a plastic or metal scraper. You know when the stripper is working because the surface becomes crinkled. Once it is been treated with stripper, old varnish and the accumulated dirt of years come out of the chequering with a hard bristle brush such as a nailbrush. Take your time and get the very last particles of varnish out of all the nooks and crannies, then take particularly good care to follow all the instructions on the pack for 'killing' the stripper. The usual recommendation is a copious wash with white spirit, but do check.

Essential oils for stock finishing are contained in good-quality, stock-finishing kits. All you have to do is follow the instructions provided.

After the wood has dried, following any recommended washing process, sand it lightly, always working in the direction of the grain and avoiding the chequering and any areas critical to the wood-to-metal fit. After this preliminary rub you can make a careful examination for cracks and damage. Small cracks may be glued, as we have explained earlier, and dents raised.

Dents

To raise a dent you will need a flat, metal object, such as an old knife, and some cotton or flannel cloth. The cloth is soaked in water and placed over the dent and the knife is heated by holding it in a gas flame until it is a dull red hot. Press the hot blade into the area over the dent, being careful to take it off before the cloth and the wood beneath start to scorch. The steam generated in the cloth will be forced into the grain of the wood, persuading it to return to its original contours. You may have to repeat the process several times, rewetting the cloth and reheating the knife on every occasion, until the dent comes out.

With any dents removed and any cracks glued, the next step is to raise the grain of the wood so that it will eventually sand absolutely flat. This is done by sprinkling the stock with clean, cold water. Professionals dry the wood quickly in a flame, but this calls for fine judgement and a hair dryer is a lot safer.

Sanding and Filling

The serious sanding may now begin, using increasingly fine grades and – again – always working the way of the grain. Except for work in niggly corners, the paper is best held over a soft wood, hard rubber or cork block. Remember that you are trying to remove the absolute minimum amount of wood to achieve smoothness, and that to take your time with a fine paper usually does a better job than rushing things with a coarse one.

The next job depends on the nature of the wood. If it looks at all porous it is going to need a coat of filler, otherwise oil is just going to con-

This stock has been rubbed back to the bare wood and is almost ready for the grain to be raised before its final finishing.

The wood of this gun has been stripped down and lightly damped to raise the grain.

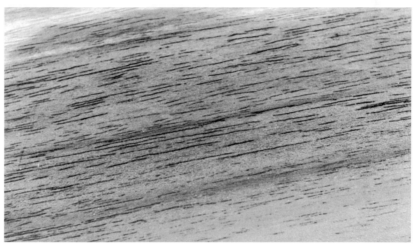

tinue soaking in and will never form a good surface finish. It is possible to buy stock fillers and they are very good, but I usually use well thinned yacht varnish to which a few spoonfuls of talcum powder have been added. Use it sparingly and remember that you are not trying to form a surface glaze with it; you are just trying to reduce the porosity by blocking the natural pores in the wood. Once the filler has dried lightly sand the stock all over again.

Colouring and Polishing

Now is the time to decide whether you want to darken the wood or change its colour – say from a yellowish shade to brown. You may use any spirit-based wood dye, but do not use a water-based one or you may raise the grain again. The traditional stocker's wood-darkening agent is alkanet root oil which may be bought from gun shops.

Once the stock is the right colour, the real polishing can begin. There are some very good stock-finishing kits on the market and I would recommend that you should get one of them and just follow the instructions rather than use doubtful samples of linseed oil. Do remember, however, that all good oils take quite a long time to dry and that drying times are extended in cold weather. The traditional 'London' oil finish takes many weeks to produce because it is built up by the application of a very large number of very thin coats and each has to be left to dry, which may take a day or more.

If you want a very quick finish with a fast-drying oil, Rustin's Teak Oil does a fair job and is available at many DIY shops. Do not paint it on, as it says in the instructions, or the layer will be far too thick. Just use a few drops at a time on a cotton pad and let it dry thoroughly before you use the gun again.

Usually, when oil has dried hard, you can improve its shine by vigorous rubbing with a cotton cloth. Do not use polishing mops in power drills or you may generate heat which will melt the surface and cause marking.

Varnishes and French Polish

Varnished finishes are not very popular in Britain and they do tend to show marks and scratches rather more than traditional oil does. However, on guns used for 'fowling or in other rigorous conditions – particularly where they are likely to get wet – varnish is highly durable and keeps out water if it is well applied. Use a good grade of marine varnish and apply the first coat well thinned. Water-based varnishes, although much advertised, are not suitable for gun stocks, and neither are the majority of varnishes which contain their own colouring agents. Rub the stock down with very fine wet-and-dry between coats and you should get an excellent finish.

An alternative is to use French polish, which consists of shellac dissolved in methylated spirits. It is best applied by using a lump of cotton wool wrapped in a non-whiskery cotton cloth. Pour a teaspoonful or more into the cotton wool, wrap the cloth around it and apply it by moving the hand in small circles. It is possible to build up several coats, and the polish has the advantage of drying much more quickly than all other finishes. But with all polishes and varnishes, do not fill up the chequering or the result will be ugly and the chequering will cease to do its job, which is to provide a secure grip.

Woodwork is a specialist job, and if you do make a mistake the damage may be difficult and expensive to rectify. For this reason it is best to take your gun to a professional if you are not totally confident about your ability.

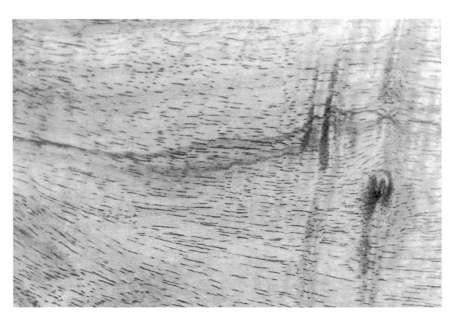

Successive coats of oil should produce a finish like this – smooth without being 'glassy', and complementary to the natural grain of the wood.

GLOSSARY

Action The part of a gun behind the barrel which contains the firing and locking mechanism.

Allen key A key of hexagonal cross-section used for driving socket-head screws.

Antimony A metal alloyed with lead for shot-making, to make the shot harder.

Bar The international unit of pressure used in gun proofing and to denote the pressure of cartridges. One bar is the normal pressure of the atmosphere at sea level.

Barrel flats The flat sections underneath the chambers, next to the lump of a side-by-side gun, usually where proof stamps are found.

Barrel loop The metal projection, beneath the barrels, to which the fore end is attached.

Barrel set The completely assembled barrel, including the ribs, sights and lumps.

Bismuth A non-toxic heavy metal with many characteristics similar to those of lead; used as a lead substitute in limited-production cartridge manufacture.

Bite Any indent in a mechanism: for instance, the indent in the part of the barrel mechanism into which the forward end of the bolt fits to lock the gun closed.

Bolt The sliding metal wedge, usually operated by the top lever, which holds the gun locked closed.

Bore The internal part of a barrel; a term also used to designate the barrel's diameter (e.g., 12-bore or 20-bore).

Boxlock A gun in which all of the mechanism is contained within a 'box' in the metal action, behind the barrels.

Break action The action of any shotgun which is loaded by breaking the barrels away from the standing breech on a hinge mechanism, to differentiate it from other actions, such as semi-automatic or pump.

Breech The chamber end of a shotgun barrel.

Buttplate The curved plate fitted to the extremity of a gun's butt; the part which fits against the shooter's shoulder.

Cast The sideways bend of a stock, usually measured at the heel and the toe. The direction of a cast determines whether the gun is left- or right-handed.

Chamber The part of the barrel at the breech end, into which the cartridge fits.

Choke The constriction in the muzzle end of a shotgun barrel which influences the pattern of shot thrown.

Chopper lump A method of barrel construction in which the lump is forged from the same piece of metal as the barrel tube (*see* Lump).

Cocking rod The rod which recocks a gun's mechanism, usually when it is opened for the insertion of fresh cartridges.

Colour hardening A hardening process for steel which produces an abstract pattern of surface colours, usually blues, browns and yellows.

Comb The top ridge of a gun's butt.

Crimp closure A method of closing the mouth of a cartridge case by means of folding the tube material.

Draw bolt The screwed bolt which attaches the butt of an O/U shotgun to the metal of the action (*see* O/U).

Drop, at heel and comb The vertical measurements between the back and the front of the comb on a stock and a line projected back from the sighting plane.

Ejector kickers A mechanism, usually within the fore-end, which causes he ejectors to operate and expel spent cartridges when the gun is opened.

Ejectors The mechanism which ejects spent cartridges when a gun is opened.

Fibre wad   A cartridge wad which is made of a natural, fibrous material which is degraded by exposure to weather.

Firing pin   The sliding metal pin which strikes the primer of a cartridge when the trigger is pulled. 'Striker' is an alternative name.

Fixed choke   Chokes which are permanently machined into the muzzles of a gun and are not removable.

Forcing cone   The tapering part of a barrel bore immediately in front of the chamber, in which the diameter is reduced from the chamber diameter to the main barrel diameter.

Fore-end   The wooden part which lies under the rearward end of the barrel or barrels and is gripped by the hand which is not operating the trigger.

Fore-end iron   The metal part within the fore-end which helps to secure the woodwork to the gun and, when in position, forms part of the gun's jointing.

Foresight   The small sight at the tip of a gun's rib.

Full-width pin   The type of hinge pin which goes right across the forward part of the action, from one wall to the other.

Gas-operated   A semi-automatic shotgun which is reloaded by a mechanism utilizing gas pressure in the barrel when the gun is fired.

Gas port   The small hole in a semi-auto barrel which leads high-pressure gases into the piston mechanism and which cycles the action.

Game gun   A gun designed for shooting game birds or for general field shooting.

Gauge   The American term for bore, as in 12-gauge and 20-gauge.

Hand   The part of the stock which is gripped by the palm and fingers of the trigger hand.

Head   The part of the stock which forms the joint with the gun's action.

Head (cartridge)   The metal head on a cartridge case: the rimmed part which contains the primer.

Headspace   The space between the cartridge head and the standing breech when the gun is closed.

Heel   The top rearmost corner of a gun's butt.

Hinge pin   The metal pin, through the action, to which the barrels are hinged.

Hook   The semi-circular cut-out in a barrel lump which fits around the hinge pin to from the jointing.

Inertia block   A mechanism for resetting the trigger of a single-trigger gun to the second barrel, utilizing the recoil of the first barrel to the fired.

Jag   A slotted cylinder of soft metal or plastic, usually with a roughened surface, around which cloth or paper may be wrapped for barrel cleaning.

Jointing   The hinge mechanism of a break-action shotgun.

Knuckle   The half-round section at the forward end of an action which forms a bearing with the fore-end iron.

Lock   The complete firing mechanism of a gun, including hammers, sears and mainsprings.

Lock Plate   The plate bearing the firing mechanism of a sidelocck gun.

Lump   The metal projection beneath the barrels which hinges on the hinge pin and also usually contains the bite into which the bolt fits.

Mainspring   The spring which drives a gun's hammer mechanism.

Mechanical trigger   A single trigger which is not reliant on recoil to reset it for the second shot in a double-barrelled gun.

Mid-rib bead   A small sighting bead at the mid-point of the top rib.

Monobloc   A method of constructing barrels by means of sleeving two separate tubes into a steel forging which forms the breech ends and the lump.

Monte Carlo   A style of stock which has a

raised cheek piece parallel to the sighting plane of the gun.

Multichoke A choke mechanism which may be varied by screwing tubes of differing internal diameter into the muzzle ends of the barrels.

Muzzle The forward end of a barrel from which the shot issues into the atmosphere.

Muzzle velocity The speed of the shot load the moment it issues from the muzzle.

Nitrobenzene An active ingredient in some powerful barrel cleaning solvents, poisonous by skin contact.

Nitrocellulose The substance from which propellant powders are made.

Nitro proof The official testing of a shotgun with modern nitro powders, as opposed to the older black gunpowder.

Observed velocity The average speed of the shot load, usually measured over the first 20m of its flight.

Olympic Trap The international trap-shooting discipline shot at the Olympic Games.

Over and under A double-barrel shotgun made with one barrel on top of the other.

O/U A common abbreviation for over and under.

Pattern The distribution of pellets in a charge of shot as it travels through the air.

Perceived recoil The recoil which the shooter feels through the gun, rather than the actual recoil forces generated by the cartridge.

Pistol grip A stock with the hand shaped like the grip of a pistol (see Hand).

Photodegradable A property of some plastic cartridge wads which are degraded by exposure to daylight.

Pitting Indentations in the inner barrel walls of a shotgun, caused by corrosion.

Primer The part of a cartridge which ignites the powder charge when struck by the firing pin.

Proof The official testing of a shotgun for safety at a legally-recognized testing station, known as a proof house.

Propellant The powder which, as it burns, provides the gas pressure which causes a gun to fire.

Pump-action A reloading system for a repeating shotgun actuated by sliding the fore-end back and forth.

Ramped rib An elevated rib, rising from the barrels, with a ramp at its rear end.

Recoil The backward force of a gun caused by a shot being fired.

Recoil-operated A semi-automatic shotgun which is reloaded from the magazine by the recoil of a shot being fired.

Recoil pad A pad fixed to the butt of a gun so that, when pressed to the shooter's shoulder, it helps to absorb and dissipate the recoil forces.

Rib Usually the sighting plane along the top of a gun's barrel or between the barrels of a side-by-side; side ribs are fitted between the barrels of an O/U (see O/U).

Safety thumbpiece The button used to activate the safety catch, usually positioned so that it can be moved by the thumb of the trigger hand.

Sear The part of a gun's mechanism which holds back the hammer when the action is cocked. The trigger mechanism moves the sear to cause the gun to fire.

Selective trigger A single-trigger mechanism which can be set to fire the barrels of a double-barrelled gun in the order predetermined by the shooter.

Semi-auto A single-barrelled magazine shotgun, reloaded by the force of the first shot being fired.

Side-by-side A double-barrelled gun with the barrels arranged in an horizontal plane.

Sidelock A gun with the lock mechanism or mechanisms, set into separate, removable plates which are attached to the sides of the action.

Side plate An artificial lock plate fitted to a boxlock gun for cosmetic purposes.

Skeet A clay shooting discipline in which crossing targets from towers are tackled from firing points around a half circle.

Skeet gun   A gun designed specifically for the skeet discipline, usually with very open chokes.

Sleeved   A gun which has had new barrel tubes fitted to the original breech ends is said to be 'sleeved'.

Sporter   A gun designed for the several different sporting disciplines within clay shooting.

Sporting   A clay shooting discipline with a wide variety of targets intended to simulate field shooting situations.

Spring-loaded ejectors   Ejectors which are under constant spring pressure and held down by a mechanism which is released when the gun is opened after firing.

Standing breech   The part of the action immediately behind the barrels which closes with the cartridge heads when the gun is closed and contains the firing pins.

Striker   Another term for a firing pin.

Stub pins   The short hinge pins of a low-profile action, protruding from within the forward ends of the action walls and locating with semi-circular cut-outs machined into the chamber walls.

Superposed   Another term for an over and under gun.

S/S   The usual abbreviation for side-by-side.

Toe   The lower, most rearward point of a gun's stock.

Top lever   The top-mounted opening lever of a break-action shotgun.

Top strap   The top, rearward part of a gun's action, behind the top lever, usually carrying the safety thumbpiece.

Trap   One of many clay disciplines in which shooters tackle angled, going-away targets from behind the trap house. Examples are down the Line, Automatic Ball Trap and Olympic Trap.

Trap gun   A shotgun specifically designed for the trap disciplines.

Trigger plate   The plate forming the lower part of a gun's action, to which the trigger mechanism and, usually, most of the other parts of the firing mechanism are attached.

Tumbler   Another term for a hammer.

Turnscrew   A gunsmith's term for a screwdriver.

Ventilated rib   A rib with cut-out sections, for good heat dissipation and lightness.

Wad   The material underneath the shot in a cartridge which drives the shot through the barrel and forms a gas seal against the pressures of the burning powder.

Wildfowling gun   A gun designed for shooting ducks, geese and other wildfowl.

INDEX